A Slice of ORANGE

Favorite  Recipes

Honorary Cookbook Co-Chairmen:
John Ward
Pat Johnson

Cookbook Steering Committee:
Jackie McInnis, College of Human Ecology, Coordinator
Tom Mattingly, UT Sports Information
Susan Williams, Lady Vols
Carol Evans, Lady Vols
Sarah DeYoung, College of Human Ecology

Committee Members:
Michelle Hanson, Lady Vols
Carol Costello, College of Human Ecology
Janis Brickey, College of Human Ecology
Melinda Sutton, College of Human Ecology
Nancy Starnes, a true "Volunteer"

"The Hill and Beyond," the cover art for this cookbook, was painted and donated by East Tennessee artist Trina Sales. Signed and numbered limited edition prints of the original oil painting are available from the Tennessee Traditions Store (615-974-1270) on the UT campus. The size of the print is 11 inches by 28 inches. Framed prints are available through the artist by contacting the Tennessee Traditions Store.

Photographs in the book have been provided by UT Photographic Services; UT Sports Information; Bill Shipley of the *Chattanooga Free Press*; Glenn Thackston of the UT Sports Information Office, now with the Southeastern Conference; *The Orlando Sentinel*; and Janis Brickey of the College of Human Ecology.

This cookbook is a collection of favorite recipes, which are not necessarily original recipes.

Published by: The University of Tennessee, Knoxville
                UT College of Human Ecology
                UT Men's Athletic Department
                UT Women's Athletic Department

Copyright© The University of Tennessee
            Knoxville, Tennessee

Library of Congress Number: 95-60116
ISBN: 0-87197-421-5

Designed, Edited, and Manufactured by:
Favorite Recipes® Press
P.O. Box 305142
Nashville, Tennessee 37230
1-800-358-0560

Manufactured in the United States of America
First Printing: 1995   20,000 copies

ORANGE NOTES

Big Orange Country is really a way of life. *A Slice of Orange* is food for thought from many of the people who have brought life to Big Orange Country. Take time to share the celebrations, anecdotes, and most of all, the recipes of Big Orange citizens. Some of the ideas may be as exciting as a Big Orange football or basketball game! Probably not. But at least you can try.

John Ward
Honorary Co-Chair

A Slice of Orange is the product of the efforts of many people. The early support and cooperation of Doug Dickey, Director of Men's Athletics, Joan Cronan, Director of Women's Athletics, and Jacky DeJonge, Dean of the College of Human Ecology, were instrumental to the successful completion of the project. We are particularly grateful to all the individuals who contributed their recipes. Without them, this book would not have been possible. To those of you who bought the book go our heartfelt thanks. A special thanks goes to Nancy Starnes, who volunteered many hours categorizing recipes. The proceeds from this book will help provide student scholarships in Women's Athletics and the College of Human Ecology.

Pat Johnson
Honorary Co-Chair

INTRODUCTION

This book just needed to happen! As the University of Tennessee enters its third century, many of these collective memories needed to be shared or perhaps might have been lost forever! This has been a joint venture between the Men's Athletics Department, the Women's Athletic Department, and the College of Human Ecology.

The social atmosphere surrounding sports activities at major universities is an important part of the American scene, particularly at UT. The University has a rich reputation, both academically and in athletics, and this cookbook focuses on a unique part of University life. This is really a storybook, a collection of favorite recipes from UT fans of all walks of life. Included are recipes from University presidents, faculty, alumni, athletes, parents, and friends. Many of them have shared their UT memories, which we are happy to share with you. This is a book to be used and enjoyed.

This book is not intended to present a comprehensive picture of the University's total sports program nor of the individuals who have contributed to its rich history. Because of the social aspects of food and fellowship surrounding football games, the emphasis naturally falls upon the gridiron. Friends and families gather in the fall to share in the festivities of tailgating and socializing. What one contributes to the tailgate party often has a competitiveness to it as well, and recipes are tried and shared among the group. Planning and packing for the event is not to be left to chance or to the last minute. For some, going to the tailgate party is the highlight of the day.

College sports provide the opportunity for a lot of fun, fellowship, and memories. In developing the concept for this book, we tried to depict some of this by sharing recipes, stories, and pictures of events at the University of Tennessee. We hope the reader will get a feel for what makes college sports unique to fans and the sense of rich traditions at UT. Our stars, fans, and alumni have contributed some very good recipes. We hope you enjoy this slice of "Big Orange Country."

CONTENTS

TENNESSEE FOOTBALL TRADITION

Tradition is a wonderful thing, particularly the 104-year-plus tradition of Tennessee football. You can't manufacture it and nobody really knows how to define it, but you know it when you see it. And, perhaps, more importantly, you know it when you feel it.

It's a tradition of winning. Tennessee is the 10th winningest team in the country. UT has the winningest overall athletics program in the conference with over 100 SEC titles. In football, it has eleven SEC championships, three since 1984. It has ten NFL first-round draft choices in the past six years, 35 bowl appearances, and 125 overall television appearances.

Tennessee tradition is a distinctive shade of Orange, unmatched anywhere in college football. It's the "T's" on the side of the helmets; the "Vol Walk" before the games from Gibbs Hall to

the stadium; the Orange and White checkerboard end zones; a wave of Orange across the 91,000-seat expanse of Neyland Stadium, slated to be over 102,000 by the start of the 1996 season; the memory of W. S. Shields and Alice Watkins and grass on the floor of the field that bears their name.

Tennessee tradition is tailgating in the parking lots and hearing John Ward's pre-game show at the base of the Hill near Alumni Gym; hearing Bobby Denton say, "Please pay these prices and please pay no more;" watching the "Pride of the Southland Marching Band" marching down Volunteer Boulevard, turning right on Andy Holt Avenue and heading to the stadium; lining up against Alabama, usually on the third Saturday in October, but on the second Saturday in 1995.

Tennessee tradition is the band massed at the north end, ready to begin the nation's most exciting pre-game show, culminating when the Vols burst through the "T." It's "Rocky Top," the "Spirit of the Hill," and the "Hallowed Hill in Tennessee."

Tennessee tradition is a lineage of blue tick coon hounds named Smokey that lead the Vols through the "T." It's the memory of Rev. W. C. Brooks and the continued support of Mildred Brooks and Earl Hudson.

It's the 200-plus boat "Volunteer Navy" dotting the Tennessee River at the south end of the stadium, covering the waterfront with boats of all sizes and descriptions.

It's defense and the kicking game, the game maxims of Gen. Robert R. Neyland, and finding a way to come from behind at Notre Dame in 1991 to win 35-34. It's Orange and White flags on the windows of automobiles and vans on I-40, I-75, or any other road leading to where the Vols play.

That's the way it's been with University of Tennessee football over the years, as it continues to provide Vol fans with memories for the ages.

Tennessee football occupies a special place in the hearts and minds of Tennessee fans, regardless of when and where they saw their first Vol game.

It's a year-round subject of discussion in barbershops, on church steps, or any place Vol fans get together.

But more than anything, tradition is really a sense of *deja vu*, that fancy term for the feeling you get when you think you've been there before.

It's great players, coaches, and plays. It's the inevitable comparisons, the frames of reference fans bring to the game. It's the thrill of being a part of something that unites the State of Tennessee as nothing else can.

It's remembering Gene McEver returning a kickoff against Alabama in 1928; a run by Johnny Butler in 1939; Dick Huffman against Harry Gilmer in 1946. Hank Lauricella against Texas in the 1951 Cotton Bowl; Albert Dorsey's interception against Alabama in 1967; Johnnie Jones emerging from the shadows to a hero's welcome at the northeast corner of Legion Field in 1983; the Superdome in New Orleans becoming Big Orange Country South in the 1986 Sugar Bowl. And much more.

When Vol defenders make a goal line stand, there's immediate reference to great goal line stands of the past. The same is true with players.

On defense, when Ben Talley or Scott Galyon flattened an opposing ball carrier, the comparisons to previous linebackers become obvious. Was the hit more reminiscent of Frank Emanuel, Steve Kiner, Jack Reynolds, or Keith DeLong?

Likewise on offense, when Jeff Smith, Bubba Miller, Jason Layman, Kevin Mays, or Leslie Ratliffe moved out opposing linemen, fans wondered how they compared with Chip Kell, Bob Johnson, Ted Daffer, or Ed Molinski. Or was Bob Suffridge better up front than anyone who ever wore an Orange shirt? Who can say?

That's the beauty of it all. The comparisons are endless, but that's all part of tradition. Great players and great plays live on in the mind's eye, to be recalled at a moment's notice.

As former Vol Tim McGee, now a stickout wide receiver in the pros, once said: "It's a Super Bowl atmosphere every Saturday at Neyland Stadium." But you already knew that.

Thomas J Mattingly

Tom Mattingly (1970, 1977)
Editor of *Volunteers Magazine*

ORANGE SUNRISE

One of the most popular dishes for any Tennessee brunch is country ham. Dr. W J Julian shares this method of cooking country ham:

Bring the shank end of a Hickory Farms country ham to a simmer in water to cover in a very large stockpot. Simmer by "letting the water smile" for about 3 hours. Let stand in the water overnight or until cool. Trim off most of the fat. Score the top, stud with cloves and sprinkle with freshly ground pepper. Broil just until the top is brown.

Dr. Julian joined the UT faculty as associate professor of music education and director of UT bands in 1961. In 1972, he introduced the song "Rocky Top" to the the band's halftime show, and it became so popular that in one year it was played 500 times. Under his direction, the Pride of the Southland Band was consistently rated among the top marching groups in the country. Dr. Julian retired in 1993.

Ruth DeFriese (1934, 1958) gives us her recipe for country ham and red eye gravy:

Slice the ham from 1/4 to 3/8 inch thick. Score the fat edges to prevent buckling. Place in a warmed heavy skillet. Cook slowly over medium heat, turning slices frequently; do not cover. Avoid overcooking, which makes ham tough; it is usually done when the fat browns. Remove the ham to a warm serving platter. Heat the juices and fat from ham in a skillet over high heat. Add 1/4 cup water for every 4 slices of

BACON WRAPS

Makes 30

10 slices bread
1 (8-ounce) jar process cheese spread
10 slices bacon, cut into thirds

Remove crusts from bread; cut lengthwise into thirds. Spread with cheese spread. Roll up to enclose filling. Wrap bacon around rolls; secure with wooden picks. Place on baking sheet.

Bake at 400 degrees for 15 to 20 minutes or until bacon is cooked through.

Mary Ann Harding, Germantown, Tennessee

SAUSAGE MUFFINS

Makes 12

6 English muffins, split
1 pound hot sausage
2 (5-ounce) jars Old English cheese spread
6 tablespoons margarine, softened

Place English muffins cut side up on baking sheet. Brown sausage in skillet, stirring until crumbly; drain. Combine sausage, cheese spread and margarine in bowl; mix well. Spread on muffins.

Bake at 400 degrees for 7 minutes.

You may freeze unbaked muffins on a baking sheet and then remove to freezer bags. Bake at 400 degrees for 7 minutes. Cut each muffin into four wedges with a pizza cutter for appetizers, or leave whole for a snack.

Trish Harrison, Greeneville, Tennessee

MUSHROOM TURNOVERS

Makes 50

8 ounces cream cheese, softened
1 cup butter, softened
2 1/4 cups flour
1 teaspoon salt
Mushroom Turnover Filling
1 egg, beaten

Combine cream cheese, butter, flour and salt in bowl; mix well. Knead until soft dough forms. Shape into ball. Chill, wrapped, for 2 hours.

Roll dough 1/8 inch thick on floured board. Cut with 1-inch cookie cutter. Place 1 teaspoon Mushroom Turnover Filling on each round. Fold in half. Press edges with fork, dampening fork as needed. Brush with beaten egg. Place on baking sheet sprayed with nonstick cooking spray.

Bake at 325 degrees for 30 minutes or until golden brown.

Mushroom Turnover Filling

8 ounces mushrooms, chopped
1 large onion, chopped
1/4 cup sour cream
1 tablespoon flour
3 tablespoons butter, softened
1/4 teaspoon thyme
1/2 teaspoon salt
1/2 teaspoon pepper

Combine mushrooms, onion, sour cream, flour and butter in bowl; mix well. Stir in thyme, salt and pepper.

Mrs. Ollie Keller, Nashville, Tennessee

Ollie Keller, who played UT football in 1950 and 1951, says that General Neyland was the greatest coach of all time and that UT is the greatest university.

STRAWBERRIES WITH SPICES

Serves 4

1 (6-ounce) glass of red wine
1/8 teaspoon cinnamon
1/8 teaspoon ginger
1/4 cup sugar
8 ounces strawberries

Combine wine, cinnamon, ginger and sugar in saucepan; mix well. Cook until heated through; do not boil. Let stand until cool. Rinse strawberries; remove leaves. Place in large bowl. Pour wine mixture over strawberries. Chill for 1 hour.

Daedra Charles, Detroit, Michigan

TENNESSEE CAVIAR

Serves 30

3 (15-ounce) cans black-eyed peas, drained
1 large green bell pepper, chopped
1 large onion, chopped
1/2 cup chopped jalapeño peppers
1/2 cup hot salsa
1/4 cup cider vinegar
3/4 cup sliced green olives
3/4 cup Italian salad dressing
2 bay leaves
1 teaspoon salt

Combine peas, green pepper, onion, jalapeños, salsa, vinegar, olives and salad dressing in bowl; mix well. Stir in bay leaves and salt. Chill, covered, overnight. Remove bay leaves. Serve with dip-size corn chips.

■ This is great for any gathering, but it's especially good for New Year's Day bowl games when you want the good luck that black-eyed peas bring!

Sarah DeYoung, Maryville, Tennessee
Director, Advising Center, College of Human Ecolog

Daedra Charles is the latest Lady Vol basketball player to have her jersey retired, playing at UT from 1988 to 1991. She was the first SEC player to win the Wade Trophy, the highest honor in women's basketball. Daedra graduated from UT with a degree in child and family studies and is currently playing professional basketball in France.

13

Kelli was a Lady Vol basketball player from 1988 to 1992. She lists these as some of her favorite memories: going to Hawaii; seeing Pat dance on a table after winning the 1989 National Championship in Tacoma, Washington; touring the White House and meeting President Bush in 1991; winning their second—and Pat's third—National Championship in New Orleans; and going to London and claiming to have seen the Queen as she gave her famous wave. Kelli is the coach of women's basketball at Maryville College.

PINEAPPLE CHEESE BALL

Serves 12

        16 ounces cream cheese, softened
        1 (8-ounce) can crushed pineapple, drained
        1/4 cup grated green bell pepper
        2 1/2 tablespoons grated onion
        1 tablespoon seasoned salt
        1 cup chopped pecans

Combine cream cheese, pineapple, green pepper, onion and seasoned salt in bowl; mix well. Spoon into small bowl lined with plastic wrap. Chill for 1 hour.

Invert onto serving tray and remove plastic wrap. Coat with pecans. Serve with party crackers.

Kelli Casteel Cook, Maryville, Tennessee

CRAB CANAPES

Makes 36

        1 (6-ounce) package frozen crab meat, thawed, or
          1 (7-ounce) can, drained
        1 tablespoon chopped green onions
        1 cup shredded Swiss cheese
        1/2 cup mayonnaise
        1 teaspoon lemon juice
        1/4 teaspoon curry powder
        1/2 teaspoon salt
        1 (8-ounce) can butterflake refrigerator rolls
        1 (8-ounce) can sliced water chestnuts, drained

Combine crab meat, green onions, cheese, mayonnaise, lemon juice, curry powder and salt in bowl; mix well.

Separate each roll into 3 layers, making 36 pieces. Arrange on greased baking sheet. Spoon crab meat mixture onto roll pieces. Top with 1 slice water chestnut.

Bake at 400 degrees for 12 minutes or until puffed and hot.

Mary Ruth Ellis Womack

ORANGE FLUFF

Serves 2

> 1/2 cup crushed ice
> 1/2 cup orange juice
> 1/2 cup milk
> 1 large banana, cut into chunks
> 1 packet artificial sweetener or 2 teaspoons sugar
> 2 orange slices

Place ice, orange juice, milk, banana and artificial sweetener in blender container. Process for 4 seconds. Pour into glasses. Top with orange slices.

■ This is a quick, nourishing breakfast drink before heading to the big game. The little fans love it, too.

Mrs. Keith S. Harrison (Pat Norris), Greeneville, Tennessee

SPINACH DIP

Serves 16

> 1 (10-ounce) package frozen chopped spinach
> 1 1/2 cups sour cream
> 1 cup mayonnaise
> 1 envelope dry vegetable soup mix
> 1 (8-ounce) can water chestnuts, chopped
> 3 green onions, chopped

Thaw frozen spinach; drain well. Combine with sour cream, mayonnaise, soup mix, water chestnuts and green onions in bowl; mix well. Chill, covered, until serving time.

Serve with your favorite sliced vegetables.

Kimberly Loveday, Chattanooga, Tennessee

Pat has vivid memories of UT in the 1950s, and her years at Henson Hall and Jennie Armstrong with the beloved Mrs. Mac. "I remember how hot we students were at the football games in our new fall outfits and seeing the alumni coming back dressed in heels, suits and sometimes hats and corsages; yet it *always* seemed to snow and freeze for the Kentucky games! I remember the UT band in their white uniforms, the sorority and fraternity dances, the UT Beauty Ball in the old gymnasium, the pep rallies, and so many other school activities. Of course, the E & E Drug Store was *the* place to see everyone and the Tennessee Theater was the place to see the good movies."

UT

June Oaks is reminded of another UT cookbook, one published by the Animal Science Wives Club in 1975, when her husband was a graduate student. She remembers many nights of burning the midnight oil typing the recipes in Morgan Hall. "The work was hard, the hours long, and the confusion great, but the endeavor provided memories enough to last a lifetime and a cookbook which I still use. As I remember, our cookbook sold out immediately and was reprinted once; but then after we all graduated, the Animal Science Wives Club eventually disbanded. We recently gave several scholarships to female agriculture students with the money that had been sitting in a Knoxville bank for all those years."

ELEGANT SALAD

Serves 12

1 head each romaine and iceberg lettuce, torn
1 (10-ounce) can artichoke hearts, drained, cut into quarters
1 (10-ounce) can hearts of palm, sliced
1 large red onion, sliced into rings
1 (4-ounce) can chopped pimento
$1^1/2$ cups grated Parmesan cheese
Salt and freshly ground pepper to taste
$1/2$ cup each olive oil and vinegar

Combine lettuce, artichoke hearts, hearts of palm, onion, pimento, cheese, salt and pepper in serving bowl. Toss with mixture of olive oil and vinegar.

June Oaks, Springfield, Tennessee

SPICED PEACH SALAD

Serves 12

1 (29-ounce) can peach halves
1 (6-ounce) package orange gelatin
$1/2$ cup sugar
1 teaspoon cinnamon
$1/4$ teaspoon ground cloves
2 cups boiling water
$1/4$ cup vinegar
$1/2$ cup each mayonnaise and sour cream
1 cup whipped topping

Drain and chop peaches, reserving juice. Mix gelatin, sugar, cinnamon and cloves in bowl. Stir in boiling water until dissolved. Add vinegar, reserved peach juice and peaches; mix well. Spoon into 9x13-inch dish. Chill until partially set. Stir to mix well. Chill until set.

Combine mayonnaise, sour cream and whipped topping in bowl; mix well. Spread over congealed layer. Chill until serving time.

Mary Nelle Moreland, Signal Mountain, Tennessee

EGGS AND CHIPPED BEEF

Serves 12

4 slices bacon, chopped
8 ounces dried beef, chopped
1 (8-ounce) can mushrooms, drained
1/4 cup butter
1/2 cup flour
1 quart milk
Pepper to taste
16 eggs
1/4 teaspoon salt
1 cup evaporated milk
1/4 cup melted butter

Sauté bacon in skillet until crisp; do not drain. Add dried beef, mushrooms and 1/4 cup butter. Stir in flour, milk and pepper. Cook until thickened and smooth, stirring constantly; set aside.

Combine eggs, salt and evaporated milk in bowl; beat well. Scramble in melted butter in large heavy skillet.

Layer 1/3 of the meat mixture and 1/2 of the egg mixture in buttered round 2-quart casserole. Repeat layers. Top with remaining meat mixture.

Bake, covered, at 275 degrees for 1 hour.

Ann Blackistone, Atlanta, Georgia

UPSIDE-DOWN HAM CASSEROLE

Serves 6

3 tablespoons margarine, softened
3 tablespoons dark brown sugar
1 teaspoon prepared mustard
1 (8-ounce) can sliced pineapple, drained
2 1/2 tablespoons flour
1/8 teaspoon pepper
1 1/2 cups quick-cooking rice
1 cup water
1/2 teaspoon salt
1 1/2 teaspoons minced onion
1 cup milk
4 slices cooked ham

Combine margarine, brown sugar and prepared mustard in 5x9-inch baking dish. Place in 400-degree oven until margarine is melted. Top with pineapple. Return to oven while preparing rice.

Combine flour, pepper, rice, water, salt, onion and milk in saucepan. Bring to a boil; reduce heat. Simmer, covered, for 5 minutes, stirring occasionally.

Remove baking dish from oven. Arrange ham over pineapple. Spread rice mixture over top. Bake, covered, at 400 degrees for 10 minutes. Let stand for 5 minutes. Invert onto serving platter.

Sue Shepherd, Crossville, Tennessee

EGG AND HAM CASSEROLE

Serves 6

6 hard-cooked eggs
1/4 cup finely chopped celery
1 tablespoon mayonnaise
1 teaspoon prepared mustard
6 slices cooked ham
1 (10-ounce) can cream of mushroom soup
1/3 cup milk
1/2 cup shredded Cheddar cheese
1/4 cup crushed potato chips

Slice eggs into halves; remove yolks. Combine yolks, celery, mayonnaise and mustard in bowl; mix well. Refill egg whites with mixture; put halves together again.

Wrap 1 ham slice around each egg. Place in baking dish. Pour mixture of mushroom soup and milk over eggs. Sprinkle with cheese and potato chip crumbs. Bake at 350 degrees for 30 minutes. Garnish with olive slices.

Anna-Lee G. Cockrill, Nashville, Tennessee

TENNESSEE SPRING BRUNCH CASSEROLE

Serves 8

9 or 10 thin slices whole wheat or white bread
1 cup chopped cooked ham
1 large onion, chopped
8 ounces mozzarella cheese, shredded
6 eggs
1 3/4 cups milk
1/4 cup bourbon or other whiskey
3/4 teaspoon salt
1/4 teaspoon black pepper
1/8 teaspoon cayenne pepper

Cut bread into quarters. Arrange half the bread in shallow 2-quart casserole. Sprinkle with half the ham, onion and cheese. Repeat layers.

Combine eggs, milk, bourbon, salt, black pepper and cayenne pepper in bowl; mix well. Pour over layers. Let stand for 5 minutes or chill for 8 to 12 hours.

Bake at 375 degrees for 30 to 35 minutes or until puffed and golden.

Shirley Sanders, Powell, Tennessee
Retired Staff, College of Human Ecology

SAUSAGE AND CHEESE CASSEROLE

Serves 8

> 1 pound sausage
> 2 cups noodles, cooked
> 1 (2-ounce) jar chopped pimento
> 1 (10-ounce) can cream of chicken soup
> 1/2 cup shredded Cheddar cheese
> 3/4 cup milk
> 1 1/2 cups cracker crumbs

Brown sausage in skillet, stirring until crumbly; drain. Add noodles, pimento, soup, cheese and milk; mix well. Spoon into casserole. Sprinkle with cracker crumbs.

Bake at 350 degrees for 15 to 20 minutes or until bubbly.

Sharon Downs, Crossville, Tennessee

SAUSAGE AND EGG BRUNCH

Serves 10

> 2 1/2 cups herb-flavored croutons
> 2 cups shredded Cheddar cheese
> 1 1/2 pounds link sausage, cooked, cut into bite-size pieces
> 8 eggs
> 2 1/4 cups milk
> 1/4 teaspoon salt
> 1/8 teaspoon pepper
> 1 (10-ounce) can cream of mushroom soup
> 1/2 cup milk

Layer croutons, 1 1/2 cups cheese and sausage in greased 9x13-inch baking pan. Combine eggs, 2 1/4 cups milk, salt and pepper in bowl; beat well. Pour over layers. Chill for 8 hours or longer. Pour mixture of soup and 1/2 cup milk over layers. Sprinkle with remaining 1/2 cup cheese.

Bake at 300 degrees for 1 1/2 hours.

Barbara McCurry Morgan (1976, 1981), Rutledge, Tennessee

VOL GUEST BREAKFAST

Serves 10

    1 pound pork sausage
    2 or 3 slices bread, cubed
    1 cup shredded Cheddar cheese
    6 eggs
    2 cups milk
    1 teaspoon salt

Brown sausage in skillet, stirring until crumbly; drain. Layer bread cubes, sausage and cheese in 9x13-inch baking dish.

Beat eggs with milk and salt in bowl. Pour over layers. Chill for 8 hours or longer.

Bake at 350 degrees for 45 minutes to 1 hour or until bubbly.

Reva McKnight Beesley, Knoxville, Tennessee

The recipe for Vols' Real-Man Quiche is submitted in memory of Dr. William Saxon Poarch, an avid Vol fan and UT alumnus, who passed away in 1994.

VOLS' REAL-MAN QUICHE

Serves 8

    1 pound sausage
    1¹/2 cups shredded Swiss cheese
    1 unbaked (9-inch) deep-dish pie shell
    1/4 cup each chopped green and red bell pepper
    2 tablespoons chopped onion
    1 cup whipping cream
    4 eggs, lightly beaten

Brown sausage in skillet, stirring until crumbly; drain. Mix with cheese. Spoon into pie shell.

Combine green pepper, red pepper, onion and whipping cream in bowl; mix well. Stir in eggs. Pour over sausage mixture.

Bake at 375 degrees for 40 to 45 minutes or until bubbly. Cool for 10 minutes. Cut into wedges. Serve warm or cold.

Paul and Nancy Hopkins, Lewisburg, Tennessee

SOUPER EASY QUICHE

Serves 8

- 1/2 cup cooked broccoli, spinach or asparagus
- 1/2 cup chopped cooked chicken, ham or turkey
- 1 cup shredded Cheddar cheese
- 1 unbaked (9-inch) pie shell
- 4 eggs
- 1 (10-ounce) can mushroom, cheese, onion or celery soup
- 1 cup milk or sour cream

Layer broccoli, chicken and cheese in pie shell. Beat eggs in bowl until foamy. Add soup and milk gradually; mix well. Pour over layers in pie shell.

Bake at 350 degrees for 50 minutes or until center is set. Let stand for 10 minutes.

Your choice of soups, vegetables, meats and cheese makes this quiche infinitely variable.

Irene Galloway, Kenton, Tennessee

ARTICHOKE AND CHICKEN CASSEROLE

Serves 8

- 4 or 5 chicken breasts, cooked, chopped
- 2 (16-ounce) cans artichoke hearts, drained
- 1 1/2 cups shredded sharp Cheddar cheese
- 1 (6-ounce) can mushrooms, drained
- 1 (10-ounce) can cream of mushroom soup
- 1 (10-ounce) can cream of chicken soup
- 1 cup mayonnaise
- 3 or 4 slices bacon, crisp-fried, crumbled

Combine chicken, artichoke hearts, cheese, mushrooms, soups and mayonnaise in bowl; mix well. Spoon into baking dish. Sprinkle with bacon.

Bake at 350 degrees for 40 minutes.

Pam Fitzhugh (1973), Ripley, Tennessee

23

CHICKEN AND CRAB MEAT CASSEROLE

Serves 6

1/2 cup sliced fresh mushrooms
1/4 cup chopped onion
3 tablespoons butter
3 tablespoons flour
1/2 teaspoon salt
1/8 teaspoon pepper
1 1/2 cups chicken broth
1/2 cup dry white wine
2 egg yolks, beaten
1 cup frozen peas
1 (6-ounce) package frozen crab meat or 1 (7-ounce) can
1/2 cup whipping cream, whipped
3 chicken breasts, cooked, chopped
1/4 cup grated Parmesan cheese
Paprika to taste

Sauté mushrooms and onion in butter in skillet until tender. Stir in flour, salt and pepper. Add chicken broth and wine gradually. Cook until thickened, stirring constantly.

Stir a small amount of the hot mixture into egg yolks; stir egg yolks into the hot mixture. Cook for 2 minutes; remove from heat. Stir in peas and crab meat. Fold in whipped cream.

Spoon over chicken in baking dish; mix gently. Sprinkle with cheese and paprika. Bake at 325 degrees for 15 to 20 minutes or until bubbly.

■ This is elegance in an easy casserole for a special occasion, when you can indulge in a few more calories.

Jacky DeJonge, Knoxville, Tennessee
Dean, College of Human Ecology

The College of Human Ecology, like sports, has a rich history and tradition at the University of Tennessee. From one class in Domestic Science in 1897, it has developed into a college composed of 80 faculty and approximately 1800 undergraduate and graduate students. In 1985, the name was changed from Home Economics to Human Ecology, but the focus of the college continues to be upon the integrated study of the natural and social sciences to enhance the well-being of individuals and families.

CRAB MEAT BREAKFAST CASSEROLE

Serves 8

    6 slices bread, crusts trimmed
    2 tablespoons margarine, softened
    1 pound fresh crab meat
    1 1/2 cups shredded Swiss cheese
    5 eggs
    2 cups half-and-half
    1 teaspoon each salt and dry mustard

Spread bread with margarine; cut into cubes. Place in buttered 9x13-inch baking pan. Sprinkle with crab meat and cheese.

Combine eggs, half-and-half, salt and dry mustard in bowl; mix well. Pour over casserole. Chill for 8 hours or longer.

Bake at 350 degrees for 40 to 50 minutes or until bubbly.

Sandra C. Lyons (1978), Huntsville, Alabama

SEAFOOD CASSEROLE

Serves 8

    1 cup each cooked shrimp and flaked crab meat
    1 cup chopped celery
    1 each medium onion and green bell pepper, chopped
    1 cup mayonnaise
    1 teaspoon Worcestershire sauce
    1/2 teaspoon Tabasco sauce
    1/4 teaspoon salt
    1 cup butter cracker crumbs

Combine shrimp, crab meat, celery, onion and green pepper in bowl. Add mayonnaise, Worcestershire sauce, Tabasco sauce and salt; mix gently. Spoon into greased baking dish. Sprinkle with cracker crumbs.

Bake at 300 degrees for 45 minutes or until bubbly.

Barbara (Bobbi) Young, Knoxville, Tennessee
Staff, College of Human Ecology

David Keith is a graduate of the University of Tennessee and an avid Vol fan. He has performed in thirty-four films, including *An Officer and a Gentleman* and *Lords of Discipline*. He has been in five television series, in five stage productions, and in five music videos. He has written and co-written music for several of his films in addition to performing with his own country and rock bands. In 1993, he was inducted into the East Tennessee Hall of Fame for the Performing Arts.

DAVID KEITH'S FOOTBALL SEASON SATURDAY MORNING HIGH-TEST SCRAMBLED EGGS

Serves 4

3 tablespoons margarine
3 jalapeño peppers, chopped, seeded
3 green chiles, chopped, seeded
3 red chiles, chopped, seeded
2 Vidalia onions, chopped
6 eggs, beaten
2/3 cup chopped Monterey Jack cheese

Melt margarine in skillet over low heat. Add jalapeños, chiles and onions. Sauté for 3 to 5 minutes or until golden brown. Increase heat to medium.

Add eggs. Cook until eggs begin to set, stirring constantly. Stir in cheese. Cook for 1 to 2 more minutes or until cheese is melted and eggs are soft-set, stirring constantly. Remove from heat.

■ Top with your favorite salsa—mine is homemade by my Mexican housekeeper. Serve with homegrown sliced tomatoes and a glass of freshly squeezed Big Orange juice. Show up at the game ready to scream!!

David Lemuel Keith, Knoxville, Tennessee

GARLIC GRITS

Serves 10

1 cup quick-cooking grits
1 teaspoon salt
4 1/2 cups water
1 cup butter or margarine
1 (8-ounce) roll garlic cheese
2 eggs
1/2 cup milk
1/8 teaspoon cayenne pepper
1 cup cornflake crumbs

Stir grits gradually into boiling salted water in saucepan. Cook using package directions. Cool slightly. Melt butter and 3/4 of the cheese in small saucepan. Stir into grits. Beat eggs with milk in bowl. Stir in pepper. Add to grits; mix well.

Spoon into greased 3-quart baking dish. Top with crumbs and remaining cheese. Bake at 350 degrees for 45 minutes.

■ This dish has accompanied my country ham for Christmas brunch for at least 20 years. In good years, it is again prepared for the bowl game on New Year's Day for the invited or drop-in crowd. It holds well warm and freezes well. Do not substitute instant grits for quick-cooking grits.

Rachel P. Gregory, Lebanon, Tennessee

HOMINY CASSEROLE

UT

Vol network analyst Bill Anderson was co-captain of the 1957 Tennessee football team and played professionally for the Washington Redskins and the Green Bay Packers, playing in Super Bowl I. Since 1968, he has been the color commentator on the Vol Network and is recognized as one of the top analysts in college football. He is now in the insurance business in Knoxville.

Serves 6

2 (16-ounce) cans golden hominy
1 (10-ounce) can Cheddar cheese soup
1 (10-ounce) can cream of mushroom soup
2 tablespoons chopped pimento
1 small onion, chopped
1/2 jalapeño pepper, chopped, or 1 tablespoon jalapeño pepper juice
1 cup crushed cornflakes
1/4 cup melted margarine

John Ward and Bill Anderson

Combine hominy, soups, pimento, onion and jalapeño pepper in bowl; mix well. Spoon into 2-quart casserole. Sprinkle with cornflakes. Drizzle with margarine.

Bake at 350 degrees for 30 minutes.

Bill Anderson,
Knoxville, Tennessee

PINEAPPLE CASSEROLE

Serves 12

> 1 cup sugar
> 1 cup flour
> 2 (20-ounce) cans pineapple chunks, drained
> 2 cups shredded mild Cheddar cheese
> 1 stack butter-flavored crackers, crushed
> 1/2 cup melted margarine

Mix sugar and flour in bowl. Sprinkle into greased 8x11-inch baking dish. Layer pineapple, cheese and crumbs in dish. Drizzle with margarine.

Bake at 325 degrees for 35 minutes. Serve hot, cold or at room temperature.

Lee Williams, Knoxville, Tennessee

BUTTERMILK BISCUITS

Makes 12

> 2 cups flour
> 1 tablespoon baking powder
> 1/2 teaspoon cream of tartar
> 2 teaspoons sugar
> 1/2 cup shortening
> 1/2 teaspoon baking soda
> 3/4 cup buttermilk

Mix flour, baking powder, cream of tartar and sugar in bowl. Cut in shortening until crumbly. Stir in mixture of baking soda and buttermilk.

Knead on floured waxed paper for 11/2 minutes. Roll 3/4 inch thick on floured surface. Cut with biscuit cutter. Place on ungreased baking sheet.

Bake at 450 degrees for 12 minutes or until golden brown. Butter immediately and enjoy—it's easier than it sounds.

Mary Jane Hays, Knoxville, Tennessee

29

KOFFEE KUCHEN

Serves 9

1 1/2 cups flour
1/4 teaspoon salt
1 teaspoon baking powder
1/2 cup butter, softened
1 cup sugar
2 egg yolks, beaten
1/2 cup milk
2 egg whites, stiffly beaten
6 tablespoons flour
1/4 cup packed brown sugar
2 tablespoons butter
1/2 teaspoon baking powder

Sift 1 1/2 cups flour, salt and 1 teaspoon baking powder together. Cream 1/2 cup butter with sugar in mixer bowl until light and fluffy. Beat in egg yolks. Add flour mixture and milk alternately, beating well after each addition. Fold in egg whites. Pour into greased 8x8-inch baking pan.

Mix remaining 6 tablespoons flour, brown sugar, 2 tablespoons butter and 1/2 teaspoon baking powder in bowl. Sprinkle over kuchen.

Bake at 350 degrees for 40 to 50 minutes or until golden brown. Cut into squares.

Sherry King Boatright, Kingsport, Tennessee

SOUR CREAM AND CINNAMON COFFEE CAKE

Serves 16

   1 cup butter, softened
   1 1/4 cups sugar
   2 eggs
   1 cup sour cream
   2 cups flour, sifted
   1/2 teaspoon baking soda
   1 1/2 teaspoons baking powder
   1 teaspoon vanilla extract
   1 tablespoon cinnamon
   1/4 cup sugar
   1 teaspoon baking cocoa

Combine butter, 1 1/4 cups sugar, eggs, sour cream, flour, baking soda, baking powder and vanilla in bowl; beat well. Mix cinnamon, 1/4 cup sugar and cocoa in small bowl. Layer batter and topping 1/3 at a time in greased bundt pan. Place in cold oven.

Set oven temperature at 350 degrees. Bake for 55 minutes.

Sherry King Boatright, Kingsport, Tennessee

APPLE-PECAN BREAD

Serves 10

2 cups flour
1 tablespoon baking powder
1/2 teaspoon baking soda
1/2 teaspoon salt
3/4 cup sugar
1/4 teaspoon nutmeg
1/2 teaspoon cinnamon
3/4 cup finely chopped pecans
1 egg, beaten
1 cup applesauce
1/4 cup vegetable oil

Combine flour, baking powder, baking soda, salt, sugar, nutmeg and cinnamon in large bowl; mix well. Stir in pecans. Make well in center of mixture. Mix egg, applesauce and oil in medium bowl. Add to flour mixture, stirring just until moistened. Spoon into greased and floured 4x8-inch loaf pan.

Bake at 350 degrees for 40 to 45 minutes or until wooden pick comes out clean. Cool in pan for 10 minutes. Remove to wire rack to cool completely.

This recipe should not be doubled. If you need two loaves, make each one separately.

Betty Kington, Crossville, Tennessee

BANANA NUT LOAF

Serves 10

- 1/2 cup shortening
- 1 cup sugar
- 2 eggs
- 2 cups sifted flour
- 1 teaspoon salt
- 1 teaspoon baking soda
- 2 ripe bananas, mashed
- 1/2 cup chopped pecans

Cream shortening and sugar in mixer bowl until light. Beat in eggs 1 at a time. Add flour, salt and baking soda; beat well. Stir in bananas and pecans. Spoon into greased loaf pan.

Bake at 350 degrees for 45 minutes to 1 hour or until loaf tests done. Remove to wire rack to cool.

Sue Shepherd, Crossville, Tennessee

BUTTER BRICKLE BREAD

Serves 24

- 1 (2-layer) package butter pecan cake mix
- 1 (4-ounce) package coconut cream instant pudding mix
- 1/2 cup vegetable oil
- 2 tablespoons poppy seeds
- 4 eggs
- 1 cup hot water
- 1 teaspoon vanilla extract

Combine cake mix, pudding mix, oil, poppy seeds, eggs, water and vanilla in mixer bowl; beat at medium speed for 2 minutes. Pour into 2 large or 3 small greased and floured loaf pans.

Bake at 250 degrees for 15 minutes. Increase oven temperature to 300 degrees. Bake for 45 minutes longer or until loaves test done. Remove to wire rack to cool.

Mrs. Joe L. McClure, Jr., Jackson, Tennessee

ZUCCHINI BREAD

Serves 20

3 cups flour
2 teaspoons baking soda
1 teaspoon salt
1/2 teaspoon baking powder
1 1/2 teaspoons cinnamon
3/4 cup finely chopped pecans
3 eggs
2 cups sugar
3/4 cup vegetable oil
2 teaspoons vanilla extract
1 (8-ounce) can crushed pineapple, drained
2 cups shredded zucchini

Sift flour, baking soda, salt, baking powder and cinnamon into bowl. Stir in pecans. Beat eggs lightly in large mixer bowl. Add sugar, oil and vanilla; beat until smooth.

Stir in pineapple and zucchini. Add flour mixture, stirring just until moistened. Spoon into 2 greased and floured 5x9-inch loaf pans.

Bake at 350 degrees for 1 hour. Remove to wire rack to cool.

Theresa Allan (1975), Hartsville, Tennessee

DATE NUT MUFFINS

Serves 24

- **2 cups whole wheat flour**
- **2 tablespoons brown sugar**
- **1 teaspoon baking soda**
- **1/2 teaspoon salt**
- **2 tablespoons wheat germ**
- **1/2 cup coconut**
- **1/2 cup dry milk**
- **1/2 cup grated orange rind**
- **1 teaspoon ginger**
- **1 teaspoon cinnamon**
- **1/8 teaspoon ground cloves**
- **1/4 teaspoon nutmeg**
- **1/2 cup oats**
- **2 eggs**
- **2 tablespoons vegetable oil**
- **1/4 cup dark molasses**
- **1 1/2 cups water**
- **1/2 cup chopped pecans**
- **1 cup chopped dates**
- **2 large bananas, mashed**

Combine flour, brown sugar, baking soda, salt, wheat germ, coconut, dry milk, orange rind, ginger, cinnamon, cloves, nutmeg and oats in bowl; mix well.

Add eggs, oil, dark molasses and water; mix well. Stir in pecans, dates and bananas. Spoon into greased and floured muffin cups.

Bake at 400 degrees for 15 minutes or until muffins test done. Remove to wire rack to cool.

Hazel Spitze, Urbana, Illinois

Hazel Spitze received her doctoral degree from UT in 1961 and joined the faculty at the University of Illinois, where she was a professor and editor of the *Illinois Teacher* until her retirement in 1987. In 1989, she received the Distinguished Service Award from the American Home Economics Association, one of the highest honors to be bestowed upon a member of the profession. In 1994 she was awarded the Arch of Achievement by the College of Human Ecology.

ORANGE-PECAN WAFFLES

Serves 4

2 cups waffle mix
1¹/2 cups water
1 tablespoon canola oil
1 cup chopped pecans
Grated rind of 1 orange
Big Orange Sauce

Combine waffle mix, water and oil in bowl. Beat with rotary beater until fairly smooth. Stir in pecans and orange rind.

Spoon into preheated waffle iron. Bake using manufacturer's directions. Remove to plates. Spoon Big Orange Sauce over top.

Big Orange Sauce

¹/2 cup butter
1 cup sugar
2 eggs
1 tablespoon boiling water
¹/2 cup orange juice
2 tablespoons lemon juice
2 tablespoons grated orange rind

Combine butter, sugar and eggs in saucepan; mix well. Stir in boiling water. Cook over medium heat until butter is melted. Add orange juice, lemon juice and orange rind gradually; mix well. Cook until sauce is consistency of heavy cream.

Linda C. Lambert (1987), Dunlap, Tennessee

CORN BREAD WAFFLES

Serves 8

  1/2 cup each cornmeal and flour
  1/4 cup wheat germ
  1 tablespoon baking powder
  3/4 teaspoon salt
  3/4 cup dry milk
  1 1/2 cups water
  1 egg, beaten
  1/2 cup melted shortening or vegetable oil

Combine cornmeal, flour, wheat germ, baking powder, salt and dry milk in bowl; mix well. Stir in mixture of water and egg. Add shortening; beat until smooth.

Spoon into hot waffle iron. Bake until golden brown, using manufacturer's directions.

You may substitute 1 3/4 cups milk for the dry milk and water.

Hazel Spitze, Urbana, Illinois

PARMESAN CHEESE ROLLS

Makes 24

  2 (12-count) packages brown and serve rolls
  1/2 cup melted butter
  3 tablespoons mayonnaise-type salad dressing
  1 cup grated Parmesan cheese

Punch hole in center of each roll. Combine butter with salad dressing in bowl; mix well with fork. Add cheese; beat well with fork.

Spoon butter mixture into holes in rolls and place on baking sheet. Bake using package directions.

Do not use mayonnaise in this recipe. Rolls may be frozen before baking.

Jimmy and Lynn Duncan, Knoxville, Tennessee

John J. "Jimmy" Duncan, Jr. (1969) represents Tennessee's Second District in the U.S. House of Representatives. His father attended UT from 1939 to 1941, served as mayor of Knoxville, and was elected to the U.S. House of Representatives from 1965 to 1988. The Duncans say, "We really felt privileged to host one of the scholarship dinners for the Lady Vols."

HOMEMADE CINNAMON ROLLS

Makes 24

1 1/2 cups flour
1 envelope dry yeast
1 1/4 cups milk
1/4 cup sugar
1/4 cup margarine
1 teaspoon salt
2 eggs
2 3/4 cups flour
6 tablespoons melted margarine
1/2 cup packed brown sugar
2 teaspoons cinnamon
2 cups confectioners' sugar
1/2 teaspoon vanilla extract or lemon juice

Mix 1 1/2 cups flour with yeast in bowl. Combine milk, sugar, 1/4 cup margarine and salt in saucepan; mix well. Cook just until mixture is warm and margarine is almost melted, stirring constantly. Stir into flour mixture.

Add eggs; beat well, scraping side of bowl constantly. Stir in as much flour as possible to make a soft dough. Knead dough on lightly floured surface; shape into a ball. Place in lightly greased bowl, turning to coat surface.

Let rise, covered, for 1 to 1 1/2 hours or until doubled in bulk. Punch dough down. Divide into halves. Roll on lightly floured surface. Mix melted margarine, brown sugar and cinnamon in bowl. Spread over dough. Roll up and cut as desired. Place on greased baking sheet. Let rise for 30 minutes.

Bake at 350 degrees for 25 to 30 minutes or until lightly browned. Invert onto wire rack. Place confectioners' sugar in large bowl. Add hot water 1 teaspoon at a time until of glaze consistency. Add vanilla. Drizzle over rolls.

Rachel Inman Carpenter, Knoxville, Tennessee

UT

As a student advocate in the Student Conduct Office, Rachel would bring in cinnamon rolls for everyone to eat. They loved them! It is a great recipe.

ORANGE DESSERT LOAF

Serves 12

1 cup plus 2 tablespoons sifted flour
13/4 cups sugar
11/2 teaspoons baking powder
1 teaspoon salt
Juice of 1 orange
8 egg whites
1/4 cup vegetable oil
2 egg yolks
1/4 teaspoon cream of tartar
1/3 cup orange juice
2/3 cup water
1/4 cup cornstarch
1 to 2 tablespoons grated orange rind
11/2 teaspoons lemon juice
2 tablespoons butter
1 cup whipping cream, whipped

Sift flour, 3/4 cup sugar, baking powder and 1/2 teaspoon salt into bowl. Make well in center. Mix orange juice with enough water to measure 6 tablespoons. Add to well with 4 egg whites, oil and egg yolks. Beat until smooth; set aside.

Beat 4 egg whites in mixer bowl until soft peaks form. Add cream of tartar gradually, beating until stiff peaks form. Fold gently into batter. Spoon into ungreased 9-inch loaf pan.

Bake at 325 degrees for 50 to 55 minutes or until loaf tests done. Cool in pan for several minutes. Remove to wire rack to cool completely. Slice lengthwise into 3 even layers.

Mix 1/3 cup orange juice with 2/3 cup water in saucepan. Add 1 cup sugar, cornstarch and 1/2 teaspoon salt. Cook over moderate heat until thickened, stirring constantly. Remove from heat. Add orange rind, lemon juice and butter; mix well; cool. Stir in 1/2 cup whipped cream. Spread between layers. Chill for 2 hours or longer. Spread top and side of loaf with remaining whipped cream.

Ruth DeFriese (1934, 1958), Knoxville, Tennessee

39

BIG ORANGE DATE CAKE

Serves 15

1 (8-ounce) package dates
1 cup chopped pecans
4 cups flour
1/4 teaspoon salt
1 1/2 teaspoons baking soda
2 cups sugar
1 cup butter, softened
4 eggs
2/3 cup orange juice
2/3 cup buttermilk
1 teaspoon vanilla extract
1/4 cup grated orange rind
1/2 cup orange juice
2 cups confectioners' sugar
1/4 cup grated orange rind

Toss dates and pecans with 1/2 cup of the flour. Sift remaining 3 1/2 cups flour, salt and baking soda together. Cream sugar and butter in mixer bowl until light and fluffy. Beat in eggs. Add flour mixture to creamed mixture gradually, beating well after each addition.

Beat in orange juice and buttermilk. Fold in dates and pecans. Stir in vanilla and 1/4 cup orange rind. Spoon into greased and floured 10-inch bundt pan.

Bake at 350 degrees for 1 hour to 1 1/4 hours or until cake tests done. Cool in pan for 15 minutes. Invert onto serving plate.

Mix orange juice, confectioners' sugar and remaining 1/4 cup orange rind in bowl. Drizzle over warm cake.

Cile Henley, Knoxville, Tennessee

JAPANESE FRUIT PIE

Serves 8

    1 cup sugar
    2 eggs, beaten
    6 tablespoons butter
    1/2 cup chopped pecans
    1/2 cup each raisins and coconut
    1 teaspoon each vanilla extract and vinegar
    1 unbaked (9-inch) pie shell

Combine sugar, eggs, butter, pecans, raisins, coconut, vanilla and vinegar in bowl; mix well. Pour into pie shell.

Bake at 350 degrees for 40 minutes.

Rachel P. Gregory, Lebanon, Tennessee

LEMON CHESS PIE

Serves 8

    1/4 cup butter, softened
    1 1/2 cups sugar
    1 tablespoon flour
    3 eggs, slightly beaten
    Juice and grated rind of 1 lemon
    2 tablespoons milk
    1 teaspoon vanilla extract
    1/8 teaspoon salt
    1 unbaked (9-inch) pie shell

Cream butter and sugar in mixer bowl until light and fluffy. Add flour; mix well. Stir in eggs, lemon juice, lemon rind, milk, vanilla and salt. Spoon into pie shell.

Bake at 325 degrees for 45 to 50 minutes or just until set. Do not overbake, as pie may separate into layers.

■ This was one of the favorite recipes Wanda served in her restaurant "Maggie's For Dinner."

Wanda L. Rust, Jacksboro, Tennessee

Rachel and Kelly Gregory met in 1951, about a week after Rachel arrived at school. A sorority sister introduced them at The Tennessean, a campus restaurant. They dated for two years and then Kelly went away to Memphis to medical school and they eventually married other people. They met again in 1981, when Kelly was divorced and she was a widow, and married a year later. "We couldn't attend the football games together in school because Kelly was in the band, but we have enjoyed going since. Thank you UT. You do good matchmaking, but it sometimes takes you an awfully long time."

41

TENNESSEE TREATS

Serves 12

1 teaspoon baking powder
1/4 cup boiling water
2 cups flour
1/2 teaspoon cinnamon
1/8 teaspoon allspice
1/8 teaspoon ground cloves
1/2 teaspoon salt
2 cups packed dark brown sugar
2 eggs
2 egg whites
2 tablespoons honey
1/2 cup raisins
1/2 cup chopped dates
1/2 cup walnut pieces

Dissolve baking powder in boiling water. Sift flour, cinnamon, allspice, cloves and salt together. Combine brown sugar, eggs and egg whites in bowl; mix well. Stir in honey and baking powder mixture.

Add flour mixture gradually, mixing well after each addition. Stir in raisins, dates and walnuts. Pour into greased 8x12-inch baking pan.

Bake at 350 degrees for 30 to 40 minutes or until wooden pick comes out clean. Cut into squares while warm.

Tipper Gore, Washington, D.C.

UT

Al Gore, Jr. is a native of Carthage, Tennessee. He served as a United States representative from 1976 to 1984 and was elected to the Senate in 1984, where he served until becoming Vice-President of the United States in 1992. He established the Nancy Gore Hunger Chair of Excellence in Environmental Studies at UT to honor his late sister. Tipper is an advocate for the mentally ill.

Lindsey Nelson remembers that he devoted every waking moment to the thoughts of Vol fortunes on the gridiron. He says that "I was an odd-jobs man—like running errands, typing scouting reports, waiting on tables, tutoring scholarship athletes in freshman English, serving as a practice field guard. And then I invented a new job for myself—spotter for radio announcers, stringer for newspaper reporters.

"My journey has carried me from Columbia to Cooperstown, from the Duck River to Doubleday Field, from the mules of Pillow Park to the Mets of Shea Stadium in New York.

"Some nights now when I'm in bed, before I fall asleep, I can hear a voice that sounds strangely like my own. It says, 'Hello, everybody, I'm Lindsey Nelson with Ralph Kiner and Bob Murphy at Shea Stadium in New York.'"

The baseball facility at UT is named in honor of Lindsey. For over four decades, Lindsey Nelson, a 1941 graduate, reigned as one of the nation's leading sports broadcasters.

A 1988 inductee into the Baseball Hall of Fame and Museum in Cooperstown, New York, Nelson served as the New York Mets' lead broadcaster for 17 seasons. He later served as the voice of the San Francisco Giants for three seasons.

He was named National Sportscaster of the Year on five occasions, and has been inducted into no less than 12 halls of fame throughout the nation, including the Pro Football Hall of Fame in Canton, Ohio.

CHEESE CRISPIES

Makes 24

> 1 cup margarine, softened
> 10 ounces extra-sharp cheese, shredded
> 1/4 teaspoon cayenne pepper
> 1 teaspoon dry mustard
> 1 teaspoon salt
> 2 cups flour
> 2 1/4 cups crisp rice cereal

Cream margarine and cheese in mixer bowl until light and fluffy. Stir in pepper, dry mustard and salt. Add flour; mix well. Stir in cereal.

Shape into small balls. Place on greased baking sheet. Flatten with fork dipped in ice water.

Bake at 350 degrees for 10 to 12 minutes or just until set; do not brown.

Armistine Shepherd, Knoxville, Tennessee

CHEESE WAFERS

Makes 72

> 1 cup flour
> 1/2 teaspoon salt
> 3/4 cup chopped pecans or walnuts
> 2 cups shredded Cheddar cheese
> 1/2 cup butter, softened

Combine flour, salt, pecans and cheese in bowl; mix well. Add butter; mix well. Divide dough into 2 portions. Shape each half into 10-inch roll between sheets of waxed paper.

Chill thoroughly. Cut into 1/4-inch slices. Place on greased baking sheet. Bake at 350 degrees for 15 minutes.

Pat Head Summitt, Knoxville, Tennessee

Pat Summitt (1975) was named Lady Vol Women's basketball coach in 1973, and has led her teams to three NCAA championships, marking up 500 wins by 1994. She was co-captain of the 1976 Olympic silver-medal team and in 1984 coached the U.S. women's team to a gold medal. She was named the Naismith college coach of the year in 1987, 1989, and 1994.

45

PARTY MIX

Serves 50

6 tablespoons melted butter
4 teaspoons Worcestershire sauce
3/4 teaspoon garlic powder
6 cups mixed corn, wheat and rice Chex
1 (12-ounce) jar dry-roasted peanuts

Pour butter into shallow baking pan. Add Worcestershire sauce and garlic powder; mix well. Add cereal and peanuts, stirring until well coated.

Bake at 250 degrees for 45 minutes, stirring every 15 minutes. Spread on absorbent paper to cool.

Betty Kington, Crossville, Tennessee

TAILGATE DEVILED EGGS

Makes 12

6 hard-cooked eggs
1/4 cup mayonnaise
1 tablespoon chopped sweet pickle
1 teaspoon prepared horseradish
1 teaspoon prepared mustard
1/4 teaspoon salt
Paprika to taste

Peel eggs; cut into halves lengthwise. Mash yolks in bowl. Add mayonnaise, pickle, horseradish, mustard and salt; mix well. Spoon into egg whites. Place on serving dish. Chill until serving time. Sprinkle with paprika.

Mary Keenan, Brentwood, Tennessee

ZUCCHINI APPETIZERS

Makes 15

> 3 cups shredded zucchini
> 1 cup baking mix
> 1/2 cup chopped onion
> 1/2 cup grated Parmesan cheese
> 2 tablespoons parsley
> 1/2 teaspoon salt
> 1 clove of garlic, minced
> 1/2 cup corn oil
> 4 eggs, slightly beaten

Combine zucchini, baking mix, onion, cheese, parsley, salt, garlic, oil and eggs in bowl; mix well. Spread in greased 9x13-inch baking pan.

Bake at 350 degrees for 25 minutes or until golden brown. Cut into 1x2-inch squares. Cool slightly. Serve warm or cold.

■ I found this recipe under the cushion of an old chair I bought and reupholstered while living in New York! It is excellent. You may substitute 8 egg whites for the whole eggs.

Linda Hannaford Roth, Knoxville, Tennessee

TAILGATE WINGS

Makes 35

> 3 cups crushed white corn tortilla chips
> 2 envelopes taco seasoning mix
> 35 (or more) chicken wing sections

Combine chips and seasoning mix in bowl; mix well. Rinse chicken. Roll in chip mixture while still damp. Place on jelly roll pan sprayed with nonstick cooking spray.

Bake at 350 degrees for 20 minutes. Remove from oven. Turn pieces carefully. Bake for 15 to 20 minutes longer or until cooked through. Serve hot with dipping sauce or salsa.

Debbie Meade Cope, Morristown, Tennessee

MINIATURE CHICKEN PUFFS

Makes 12

- 1/2 cup butter
- 1 cup water
- 1 cup flour, sifted
- 3 eggs
- 1 (12-ounce) can chicken
- 1 cup chopped celery
- 1 cup low-fat mayonnaise
- 1 tablespoon onion salad dressing mix
- 1/4 cup lemon juice

Bring butter and water to a boil in saucepan; reduce heat. Add flour all at once, stirring rapidly. Cook until mixture thickens and leaves side of pan, stirring constantly. Remove from heat.

Add eggs 1 at a time, beating well after each addition. Beat until mixture is smooth and shiny. Drop from teaspoon onto ungreased baking sheet.

Bake at 425 degrees for 20 to 30 minutes or until browned. Let stand to cool. Combine chicken, celery, mayonnaise, salad dressing mix and lemon juice in bowl; mix well. Spoon into puffs.

Bess Hammock, Knoxville, Tennessee

MONGOLIAN MEAT STICKS

Makes 16

> **2 1/2 pounds flank steak, partially frozen**
> **1 clove of garlic, crushed**
> **1/2 teaspoon ginger**
> **1/2 teaspoon sugar**
> **1/2 teaspoon pepper**
> **2 tablespoons soy sauce**
> **2 tablespoons peanut oil**
> **2 tablespoons dry sherry**
> **2 tablespoons sesame oil**
> **1/2 cup hoisin sauce**

Slice steak diagonally 1/8 inch thick. Cut slices into pieces 1 inch long. Combine garlic, ginger, sugar, pepper, soy sauce, peanut oil, sherry, sesame oil and hoisin sauce in bowl; mix well. Add steak. Marinate in refrigerator for 24 hours; drain.

Thread steak strips onto wooden skewers. Broil 3 inches from heat source for 1 minute on each side.

■ This recipe won honorable mention in the Tennessee Beef Cookoff five years ago. We enjoy it for tailgating.

Mary Ann Harding, Germantown, Tennessee

UT

John Ward has been the "Voice of the Vols" in basketball since 1964 and in football since 1968. Ward, whose understated humor enlivens his broadcasts and helps keep the games in perspective, has been Tennessee Sportscaster of the Year twenty-five times and has hosted coaches' shows in both football and basketball. He is a member of the Tennessee Sports Hall of Fame. Both John and Barbara are graduates of the UT College of Law.

CURRIED HAM SPREAD

Serves 10

> 3 ounces cream cheese, softened
> 1 tablespoon mayonnaise
> 1/2 teaspoon each curry powder and Dijon mustard
> 2 drops of Tabasco sauce
> 2 tablespoons finely chopped sweet pickle
> 1/4 cup finely chopped celery
> 1/2 cup finely chopped green onions
> 1 1/2 cups finely chopped cooked ham
> Salt and pepper to taste

Combine cream cheese, mayonnaise, curry powder, mustard and Tabasco sauce in mixer bowl; beat well. Stir in remaining ingredients. Chill, covered, for 1 hour to overnight.

Spread on lightly buttered rye bread or take spread and bread to the tailgate for "do-it-yourself" open-face sandwiches.

Jackie McInnis, Knoxville, Tennessee
Associate Dean, College of Human Ecology

PINEAPPLE-PECAN CHEESE BALL

Serves 30

> 16 ounces cream cheese, softened
> 1 (8-ounce) can crushed pineapple, drained
> 2 teaspoons grated green bell pepper
> 1 teaspoon grated onion
> 1/2 teaspoon (or less) garlic salt
> 1 teaspoon seasoned salt
> 1 cup (or more) chopped pecans

Combine cream cheese, pineapple, green pepper, onion, salt and seasoned salt in bowl; mix well. Stir in pecans. Shape into ball. Chill thoroughly. Serve with crackers.

Roll in additional pecans or sprinkle with paprika before serving if desired.

John and Barbara Ward, Knoxville, Tennessee

CHILI CHEESE LOG

Serves 24

    16 ounces cream cheese, softened
    8 ounces sharp Cheddar cheese, shredded
    1 onion, minced
    2 teaspoons minced garlic
    1/2 teaspoon garlic salt
    1/8 teaspoon salt
    3 tablespoons Worcestershire sauce
    Chili powder to taste

Mix cream cheese with Cheddar cheese in bowl. Add onion, garlic, garlic salt, salt and Worcestershire sauce; mix well with hand mixer.

Shape into log on plastic wrap. Coat with chili powder. Chill for 8 hours or longer. Serve with crackers.

Norma and Jim Harris, Knoxville, Tennessee

Jim has served for two years as president of the Lady Vols Boost-Her Club and on the UT Athletics Board.

LAYERED NACHO DIP

Serves 15

    1 (16-ounce) can refried beans
    1/2 envelope taco seasoning mix
    1 (8-ounce) container onion dip
    1 cup sour cream
    1 (4-ounce) can black olives, chopped
    2 large tomatoes, chopped, drained
    1 small onion, finely chopped
    1 (4-ounce) can chopped green chiles
    1 1/2 cups shredded Monterey Jack or Cheddar cheese

Combine refried beans with seasoning mix in bowl; mix well. Spread in 9x13-inch glass dish.

Layer onion dip, sour cream, olives, tomatoes, onion, chiles and cheese over bean mixture. Serve with corn chips.

Julia A. Davis, Talbott, Tennessee

CRUNCHY CHEESE BALL

Serves 12

8 ounces cream cheese, softened
1/4 cup mayonnaise
2 (7-ounce) cans chunky ham
2 tablespoons chopped parsley
1 teaspoon minced onion
1/4 teaspoon dry mustard
1/4 teaspoon hot pepper sauce
1/2 cup chopped peanuts

Beat cream cheese with mayonnaise in mixer bowl until smooth. Add ham, parsley, onion, dry mustard and pepper sauce; mix well.

Chill, covered, for several hours. Shape into ball. Roll in peanuts.

You may omit the peanuts and roll in dried parsley and minced onion if preferred.

Lee Williams, Knoxville, Tennessee

Annie was president of the UT National Alumni Association in 1991 and 1992. She is a graduate (1942) of the College of Home Economics.

CHILE AND OLIVE DIP

Serves 16

1 (4-ounce) can chiles, chopped
2 (4-ounce) cans black olives, chopped
4 green onions, chopped
3 tomatoes, chopped
2 tablespoons wine vinegar
1 tablespoon oil
Salt and pepper to taste

Combine chiles, olives, green onions and tomatoes in bowl; mix well. Stir in vinegar and oil. Season with salt and pepper.

Chill, covered, for 24 hours. Serve with corn chips.

Annie Martin Mitchell, Sparta, Tennessee

STUFFED CHEESE BREAD

Serves 14

1 round loaf French bread
2 cups shredded sharp Cheddar cheese
8 ounces cream cheese, softened
1 cup sour cream
1 tablespoon Worcestershire sauce
1 bunch green onions, chopped
1 (3-ounce) jar dried beef, chopped

Slice top from bread. Remove bread from loaf and tear into pieces, reserving shell. Wrap bread pieces in foil.

Combine cheese, cream cheese, sour cream, Worcestershire sauce, green onions and beef in bowl; mix well. Spoon into bread shell. Replace top; wrap in foil. Place on baking sheet.

Bake at 350 degrees for 1 hour. Place wrapped bread pieces in oven with stuffed loaf. Bake for 30 minutes longer. Place loaf on serving tray; remove top. Serve with baked bread pieces and/or crackers.

■ This is great for a tailgating party—it will stay warm for almost an hour after being taken from the oven.

Mary Ann Harding, Germantown, Tennessee

According to Rick, "The best games that I personally have attended include the 1986 Sugar Bowl, New Orleans, UT vs. Miami; the 1991 Sugar Bowl, New Orleans, UT vs. Virginia; the 1985 SEC Championship Game, Knoxville, UT vs. Vanderbilt; the 1985 UT vs. Auburn game, Knoxville; and the 1991 UT vs. Notre Dame game, South Bend. The very best of these were the 1986 Sugar Bowl and the 1991 Notre Dame games!"

TAILGATE FOOD

Arrive at the game three hours before kickoff and stay for two hours after the game. Tailgate foods can include cold drinks, fruits, cheeses, veggies, sandwiches, chips, dips, brownies, shrimp and other good things for all to enjoy. After the Pride of the Southland Band goes by, pack up and go to the game. You are providing an environment for friends and family (and their children) to enjoy the UT spirit at all football games—at home and away. Always wear your "Orange" game day attire!

Rick Regen, Nashville, Tennessee

53

ROCKY TOP JOY JUICE

Serves 16

  1 gallon water
  5 tablespoons instant tea mix with sugar and lemon
  1/4 cup orange breakfast drink mix
  2 tablespoons artificial sweetener
  1 cup pineapple juice

Combine water, tea mix, breakfast drink mix, sweetener and pineapple juice in large container; mix well. Serve over cracked ice or ice cubes.

■ "Big Orange" fans might want to use orange juice instead of pineapple juice!

George R. Price, Athens, Tennessee

HOT CIDER PUNCH

Serves 16

  4 cups water
  4 cups apple juice
  1 cup pre-sweetened red drink mix
  1/4 teaspoon ground cinnamon
  1/8 teaspoon ground nutmeg
  1/8 teaspoon ground cloves

Combine water, juice and drink mix in saucepan; mix well. Stir in cinnamon, nutmeg and cloves. Heat just to a boil. Serve hot.

■ This is very good for cold weather tailgate outings.

A UT Friend

TAILGATE TEA PUNCH

Serves 10

1 quart boiling water
5 tea bags
2 1/2 cups sugar
1 (12-ounce) can frozen lemonade concentrate
1 (12-ounce) can frozen orange juice concentrate
1 (12-ounce) can frozen limeade concentrate

Pour boiling water over tea bags in large saucepan; let stand to steep. Discard tea bags. Dissolve sugar in hot tea. Prepare lemonade and orange juice using package directions.

Combine tea, lemonade, orange juice and limeade concentrate in pitcher; mix well.

■ Transport to tailgate party in a gallon milk jug and serve over ice. Very refreshing!

Barbara R. Cantrell, Nashville, Tennessee

CHEESE SOUP

Serves 8

3/4 cup finely chopped carrots
2/3 cup finely chopped celery
1/3 cup finely chopped onion
1/4 cup melted margarine
1/3 cup flour
2 cups chicken broth
2 cups half-and-half
1 1/2 cups shredded sharp Cheddar cheese

Sauté carrots, celery and onion in margarine in skillet until tender but not browned. Stir in flour. Add broth and half-and-half gradually, mixing well after each addition.

Cook until mixture thickens and boils, stirring constantly. Stir in cheese. Cook until cheese is melted.

Susan Maples, Knoxville, Tennessee

Susan was serving this at a UT tailgate party when a man passed by and told them the soup smelled delicious. "We invited him to have a bowl with us. He did, enjoying every bite before going on to the game. We made a new Vol friend that day."

GUMBO

Serves 12

1/2 teaspoon salt
1/2 teaspoon garlic powder
1/2 teaspoon cayenne pepper
3 pounds boneless chicken breasts
3 quarts chicken stock
1 cup flour
1 teaspoon salt
1 teaspoon garlic powder
1 teaspoon cayenne pepper
1 cup vegetable oil
2 cups finely chopped onions
2 cups finely chopped mixed green and red bell peppers
1 1/2 cups finely chopped celery
1 pound country sausage, cooked, drained, minced
1 pound andouille smoked sausage or kielbasa sausage, cut into bite-size pieces
1 teaspoon minced garlic
12 cups Baked Rice

Susannah is the coach for the UT Women's Crew Club and is currently serving as the Lady Vols' crew coach.

Mix 1/2 teaspoon each salt, garlic powder and cayenne pepper together. Rinse chicken and pat dry. Rub with salt mixture. Place in baking pan sprayed with nonstick cooking spray. Bake at 350 degrees for 20 to 30 minutes or until lightly browned but not dry, turning once. Cut into 1/2-inch pieces; set aside.

Bring chicken stock to a simmer in large stockpot. Stir flour and 1 teaspoon each of salt, garlic powder and cayenne pepper gradually into oil in skillet over high heat, using long-handled metal whisk. Cook for 3 to 4 minutes or until dark brown, whisking constantly. Do not burn; if black specks develop, you must start again. Remove from heat. Stir in mixture of onions, bell peppers and celery. Stir until mixture stops turning darker, stirring constantly. Return to low heat. Cook for 5 minutes or until vegetables are tender, stirring constantly.

(continued)

Add mixture to stockpot by spoonfuls, whisking well after each addition. Bring to a boil; reduce heat. Stir in sausages and minced garlic. Simmer for 30 minutes. Stir in chicken. Cook for 5 minutes longer. Serve over mound of Baked Rice.

■ This traveled well to our Florida vs. Tennessee tailgate. I use two large stainless steel pots; one fits inside the other. Place a layer of newspapers on the bottom of the largest pot and the pot of gumbo on that. Pack newspapers around it between the inside pot and the outside pot. Tape the lid down so the gumbo won't slosh out! Lay newspapers over the lid; add the outside lid. The gumbo will stay hot for hours. This method works well for a pot of anything.

Baked Rice

4 cups uncooked rice
5 cups chicken stock or water
3 tablespoons finely chopped onion
3 tablespoons finely chopped celery
3 tablespoons finely chopped mixed green and red bell peppers
3 tablespoons butter or olive oil
1 teaspoon salt
1/2 teaspoon garlic powder

Combine rice, chicken stock, onion, celery and bell peppers in 9x13-inch glass baking dish; mix well. Stir in butter, salt and garlic powder.

Bake, covered with pan lid or foil, at 350 degrees for 1 hour and 10 minutes.

Do not use instant rice in this recipe. The vegetables float up and make a festive layer on the top.

Susannah Iacovino, Knoxville, Tennessee

57

EIGHT-LAYER "T" SALAD

Serves 15

1 cup sour cream
1 envelope taco seasoning mix
2 avocados, mashed
Lemon juice to taste
Garlic to taste
1 (16-ounce) can refried beans
2 jalapeño peppers, chopped
2 large onions, chopped
2 or 3 tomatoes, finely chopped
1 (4-ounce) can black olives, finely chopped
16 ounces sharp Cheddar cheese, shredded
6 to 8 orange bell peppers, chopped or sliced
4 to 6 green onions, chopped

Mix sour cream with taco seasoning mix in bowl; set aside. Sprinkle avocados with lemon juice and garlic. Layer refried beans, jalapeño peppers, onions, sour cream mixture, avocados, tomatoes, olives and cheese in 9x13-inch glass dish.

Use orange peppers to form the "T" from the UT logo over center of salad. Use green onions to indicate "end zone" areas.

Kimberly Loveday, Chattanooga, Tennessee

CHICKEN SALAD

Serves 16

> 8 cups chopped cooked chicken (cooked with 2 to 3 bay leaves)
> 2 cups chopped celery
> 1 cup sweet pickle relish
> 1 1/2 cups chopped pecans
> 2 1/2 cups mayonnaise or mayonnaise-type salad dressing

Combine chicken, celery, relish, pecans, and mayonnaise in bowl; mix well. Serve with favorite bread for sandwiches or with crackers.

Attention to refrigeration both in working quickly and in transporting to the tailgate party is quite important.

Sara Jane Price Threadgill, Milan, Tennessee

BROCCOLI DELIGHT SALAD

Serves 10

> 4 to 5 cups bite-size broccoli pieces
> 1/4 cup chopped red onion
> 10 slices bacon, crisp-fried, crumbled
> 1 cup sunflower seeds
> 1 cup raisins
> 1/2 cup mayonnaise
> 1 tablespoon vinegar
> 2 to 3 tablespoons sugar

Combine broccoli, onion, bacon, sunflower seeds and raisins in large bowl; mix well.

Mix mayonnaise with vinegar in small bowl. Stir in sugar to taste. Pour over salad. Toss well to mix. Chill until serving time.

Bess Hammock, Knoxville, Tennessee

Sara Jane has many memories: "ah, transferring to UT in '56 and living in Old Blount Hall although it was condemned; the College of Home Economics and the home management house with Dr. Gassett; getting pinned; bonfires and Johnny Majors quarterbacking; getting married and being one of two married couples graduating together in June 1958. Yep, there are lots and lots more memories. By the way, that marriage lasted until parted by George's death on March 28, 1994. At tailgate parties, we especially enjoyed having peel 'em and eat 'em shrimp with George's special cocktail sauce; washing hands with ice cubes; and squeezing lemon juice as a makeshift finger bowl."

CORN BREAD SALAD

Serves 8

> 1 (8-ounce) package corn muffin mix
> 1 pound mild sausage
> 1/3 cup chopped sweet bread-and-butter pickles
> 2 tomatoes, chopped
> 1/2 each onion and green bell pepper, chopped
> 1/2 cup light mayonnaise
> 2 tablespoons pickle juice

Prepare and bake corn bread using package directions. Cool in pan; crumble. Brown sausage in skillet, stirring until crumbly; drain.

Combine pickles, tomatoes, onion and green pepper in bowl; mix well. Stir in mayonnaise and pickle juice. Stir in sausage. Add all but 1/2 cup corn bread; mix well. Spoon into serving dish. Top with reserved corn bread. Garnish with pepper strips.

Ruth Garland, Rutledge, Tennessee
Shirley Sanders, Powell, Tennessee

SHOE PEG SALAD

Serves 16

> 1 (16-ounce) can each Shoe Peg corn, French-cut green
>   beans and tiny green peas, drained
> 2 cups chopped celery
> 1 (4-ounce) jar pimentos, drained
> 1 each onion and green bell pepper, chopped
> 1 cup sugar
> 1/2 cup oil
> 3/4 cup tarragon vinegar
> 1 tablespoon water
> Salt and pepper to taste

Mix vegetables in bowl. Mix sugar, oil, vinegar, water, salt and pepper in saucepan. Bring to a boil. Let stand to cool. Pour over vegetables. Chill, covered, for 8 hours or longer.

Barbara Pelot, Knoxville, Tennessee

In 1972, when Jackie McInnis joined the faculty of Home Economics Education and Shirley was the departmental secretary, Jackie would often tell her about tailgating at the Florida and Florida State football games. "Jackie, an FSU alumna, and Malcolm, a UF alumnus, their family, and friends rarely missed a game of either school. It sounded like a lot of fun, but even though she invited my husband and me many times to their UT tailgates here, we never really got started until the early 1980s. After just one tailgate we were hooked, and we have been tailgating with them ever since, through rain or shine, thick or thin, win or lose. We love it!!!!"

SUMMER POTATO SALAD

Serves 6

- **4 cups chopped cooked potatoes**
- **1 cup chopped celery**
- **1/2 cup chopped green onions**
- **1/4 cup sliced radishes**
- **2 tablespoons parsley flakes**
- **1 cup mayonnaise**
- **2 teaspoons prepared mustard**
- **1/2 teaspoon celery seeds**
- **1 teaspoon salt**
- **1/8 teaspoon pepper**

Combine potatoes, celery, green onions, radishes and parsley flakes in large bowl; mix well.

Mix mayonnaise, mustard, celery seeds, salt and pepper in small bowl. Add to potato mixture; mix well. Chill for several hours. Garnish with lettuce, egg and/or tomatoes.

Anne Dalton (1968), Knoxville, Tennessee

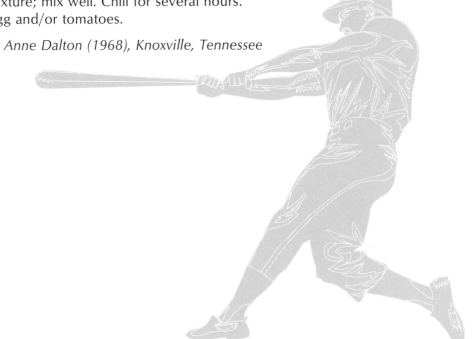

Rena is a 1959 graduate of
UT and her husband Bill
was co-captain of the 1957
Tennessee football team.
He is a several-term member
of the UT Board of Trustees,
chairing the Agriculture
Committee and serving on
the Finance and Health
Affairs Committees. He
has previously served as
Vice-Chairman of the Board
of Trustees.

TATUM ROLLS

Serves 8

1 package Tatum rolls
8 slices cooked ham
8 slices Swiss cheese
1 1/2 tablespoons prepared mustard
1 tablespoon poppy seeds
1/2 cup melted butter
1/2 teaspoon Worcestershire sauce
1 1/2 tablespoons onion flakes

Slice roll layer horizontally. Place bottom half in baking pan.
Layer with ham and cheese.

Combine mustard, poppy seeds, butter, Worcestershire sauce
and onion flakes in saucepan. Cook until heated through. Pour
half the sauce over ham and cheese. Top with remaining roll
layer. Pour remaining sauce over top.

Bake at 350 degrees for 10 to 15
minutes or until browned.

■ This is a good recipe to use for
tailgating as it doesn't have to be
piping hot.

Bill and Rena Jones Johnson
Sparta, Tennessee

GO VOLS BIG WHEEL SANDWICH

Serves 8

- **1 loaf Hawaiian bread**
- **4 ounces honey-baked ham, sliced**
- **4 ounces American cheese, sliced**
- **2 tablespoons Dijon mustard**
- **4 ounces turkey, sliced**
- **2 tablespoons mayonnaise**
- **4 ounces Swiss cheese, sliced**
- **8 ounces bacon, crisp-fried, drained**
- **1/4 cup melted margarine**
- **2 teaspoons poppy seeds**

Slice bread into 3 layers. Place 1 layer on baking sheet. Top with ham, American cheese and 1 tablespoon mustard; top with second layer of bread, turkey, mayonnaise and Swiss cheese; top with third layer of bread, bacon and 1 tablespoon mustard. Drizzle with margarine and sprinkle with poppy seeds.

Bake at 300 degrees for 25 minutes. Cut into wedges.

Ronda Byard, Clarksville, Tennessee

PEPPERONI ROLLS

Serves 12

- **1 loaf frozen bread dough, thawed**
- **8 ounces each sliced mozzarella cheese and pepperoni**
- **1 green bell pepper, sliced**
- **1 large onion, peeled, sliced**
- **8 ounces shredded Cheddar cheese**

Roll dough as thin as possible on lightly floured surface. Layer mozzarella, pepperoni, green pepper, onion and Cheddar cheese on 1/2 the dough. Fold remaining dough over, pressing to seal edges. Place on baking sheet; roll will resemble long loaf of Italian bread.

Bake using package directions. Cut into rolls.

Jessee Meade, Ocean City, Maryland

63

BLACK BEANS AND RICE

Serves 12

1 pound dried black beans
1 large onion, chopped
1 green bell pepper, chopped
1 clove of garlic, minced
1/2 cup olive oil
1 ham hock
1 bay leaf
1 teaspoon oregano
1/4 teaspoon cumin
1/2 teaspoon paprika
Salt and pepper to taste
1/2 cup vinegar

Rinse and sort beans; soak in water to cover in saucepan overnight. Add enough additional water to cover beans by 2 inches. Sauté onion, green pepper and garlic in oil in skillet. Add to beans; mix well. Add ham hock and bay leaf. Stir in oregano, cumin, paprika, salt and pepper. Bring to a boil; reduce heat to low. Cook until beans are tender.

Remove ham hock. Cut up ham; return to beans. Stir in vinegar. Cook until heated through. Discard bay leaf. Serve over white rice. Garnish with finely chopped onion.

■ Being from St. Pete, Florida, meant we often went over to Ybor City in Tampa to eat at the wonderful Spanish restaurants. This was always my favorite dish.

Malcolm McInnis, Knoxville, Tennessee
Associate Athletic Director

BAKED BEANS

Serves 8

     2 (16-ounce) cans pork and beans
     1/2 cup catsup
     1/2 cup packed brown sugar
     1 tablespoon prepared mustard
     1 tablespoon Worcestershire sauce
     1 tablespoon chili powder
     1 small onion, chopped
     1/2 teaspoon pepper
     2 slices bacon

Combine pork and beans, catsup, brown sugar, mustard, Worcestershire sauce, chili powder, onion and pepper in bowl; mix well. Spoon into 1 1/2-quart baking dish. Top with bacon.

Bake at 250 degrees for 1 hour or until bubbly and heated through.

Joe and Pat Johnson, Knoxville, Tennessee

Joseph E. Johnson (1960, 1968) was named president of UT in 1991. He is a former Chancellor of UT Memphis and was Executive Assistant to UT President Ed Boling. His wife, Pat, is a graduate of the College of Home Economics. She gives credit for the baked bean recipe to Mrs. Glen Gallion. It is a recipe Mrs. Gallion published in the UT Martin Faculty Women's Club Cookbook in 1962. No informal gathering is complete at the Johnson house without these baked beans.

REFRIGERATOR ROLLS

Serves 40

1 tablespoon sugar
1/2 cup warm water
1 envelope dry yeast
1 cup hot water
2 tablespoons sugar
1/2 teaspoon salt
5 tablespoons shortening
1 egg
4 cups sifted flour
1/4 cup melted butter

Dissolve 1 tablespoon sugar in warm water in 1-cup measure. Stir in yeast. Combine hot water, 2 tablespoons sugar, salt, shortening and egg in bowl; mix well. Let stand until lukewarm. Add yeast mixture. Add flour 1 cup at a time, mixing well after each addition.

Chill, covered, for 3 hours or longer. Roll on lightly floured surface. Shape into rolls. Place in greased 9x13-inch baking pan. Brush with melted butter. Cover with damp cloth. Let stand until doubled in bulk.

Bake at 400 degrees for 15 minutes. Rub tops with butter to keep soft. Wrap cooled rolls in foil to freeze.

Fill with ham for tailgates or picnics.

Sherry King Boatright, Kingsport, Tennessee

GRANNY RUBY'S SOUR CREAM POUND CAKE

Serves 16

3 cups flour
1/8 teaspoon salt
1 cup sour cream
1/4 teaspoon baking soda
1 cup butter, softened
3 cups sugar
6 egg yolks, beaten
1 teaspoon vanilla extract
1 teaspoon almond extract
6 egg whites, stiffly beaten
1/2 cup sifted confectioners' sugar
2 teaspoons water
1/2 teaspoon vanilla or almond extract

Sift flour and salt together 3 times. Mix sour cream and baking soda in bowl; set aside.

Cream butter with sugar in mixer bowl until light and fluffy. Beat in egg yolks 1 at a time. Add flour mixture alternately with sour cream mixture, beating well after each addition.

Fold in flavorings and egg whites. Spoon into greased and lightly floured 10-inch tube pan or bundt pan.

Bake at 300 degrees for 1 1/2 hours or until cake tests done. Cool in pan for 25 minutes. Invert onto serving plate.

Mix confectioners' sugar, water and remaining 1/2 teaspoon flavoring in bowl until of glaze consistency. Drizzle over warm cake.

■ This wonderful recipe was given to me by Ruby Hitch Thrower Baker, my aunt and my stepmother. She is one of the best cooks in Blount County and a wonderful lady.

Ann Baker Furrow, Knoxville, Tennessee

Ann Furrow is the only woman athlete ever to have played on a UT men's squad—as a member of the UT Men's Golf Team. Furrow, now the Volunteer Assistant Coach for the Lady Vols golf team, is a five-time Tennessee Women's Golf Association Champion and the first woman ever to be appointed to the University Board of Trustees, where she served for eighteen years.

CHOCOLATE CREAM CHEESE CUPCAKES

Makes 24

8 ounces cream cheese, softened
1/3 cup sugar
1 egg
1 cup chocolate chips
1 1/2 cups flour
1 teaspoon baking soda
1/2 teaspoon salt
1 cup sugar
1/4 cup baking cocoa
1 cup water
1/3 cup vegetable oil
1 teaspoon vanilla extract
1 teaspoon vinegar

Combine cream cheese, 1/3 cup sugar and egg in bowl; mix well. Stir in chocolate chips; set aside.

Combine flour, baking soda, salt, 1 cup sugar and cocoa in large bowl; mix well. Add water, oil, vanilla and vinegar; mix well. Fill paper-lined muffin cups 1/3 full with batter. Top each with 1 rounded teaspoon cream cheese mixture.

Bake at 350 degrees for 25 minutes.

■ These very moist cupcakes keep well and are easy to take along for a tailgate.

Lorraine Hensley, Greeneville, Tennessee

UT

Lorraine's favorite UT memory is a bittersweet one. "As I was coming home from a game on my sixth wedding anniversary, October 3, 1987, I fell and broke my left leg and right foot and sprained my left foot. The man who wheeled me into X-ray at Baptist Hospital said, 'Don't tell me; Reggie Cobb got hurt and they put you in to run for him.' That made me laugh and took away some of the pain."

CARAMEL CANDY

Makes 24

- **1/2 cup margarine**
- **3 cups sugar**
- **1 cup packed brown sugar**
- **3 tablespoons corn syrup**
- **1 cup evaporated milk**
- **1 teaspoon vanilla extract**

Grease top of saucepan with a small amount of the margarine to keep mixture from boiling over. Combine sugar with brown sugar in saucepan. Stir in corn syrup and evaporated milk. Add remaining margarine.

Cook to soft-ball stage, stirring occasionally; remove from heat. Beat until creamy. Stir in vanilla. Pour into buttered 9-inch dish. Let stand to cool. Cut into squares.

Ann Y. Graves, Cross Plains, Tennessee

BRICKLE BARS

Makes 24

- **1 (2-layer) package yellow cake mix**
- **1/3 cup margarine, softened**
- **2 eggs**
- **1 (14-ounce) can sweetened condensed milk**
- **1 teaspoon vanilla extract**
- **1 cup chopped pecans**
- **1/2 cup brickle baking chips**

Mix cake mix, margarine and 1 egg in mixer bowl at high speed until crumbly. Press into greased 9x13-inch baking pan.

Beat condensed milk, 1 egg and vanilla in bowl until smooth. Stir in pecans and baking chips. Pour over cake mix.

Bake at 350 degrees for 30 minutes. Let stand until center is set and cool. Cut into bars.

Hannah Crosser, Paris, Tennessee

Ann tells us that, "This recipe for Caramel Candy, like a Tennessee football tradition, has been handed down for four generations in our family. As a little girl, I can remember my grandmother making this candy at Christmas time. My mother taught me to make it and I have handed the recipe, along with being a UT fan, to my three children. It is one of their favorite treats to bring along on the ride to and from Knoxville when it's football time in Tennessee."

MOIST BROWNIES

Makes 18

1 cup vegetable oil
1 egg, beaten
2 teaspoons vanilla extract
2 cups sugar
1$^1/_2$ cups flour
5 tablespoons baking cocoa
1 teaspoon salt
1 teaspoon baking powder

Mix oil, egg and vanilla in small bowl. Combine sugar, flour, cocoa, salt and baking powder in large bowl; mix well. Stir in egg mixture. Pour into nonstick 9x13-inch baking pan.

Bake at 350 degrees for 30 minutes. Let stand to cool. Cut into squares.

You may add 1 to 1$^1/_2$ cups pecan or walnut halves to batter.

Anne Koci, Crossville, Tennessee

PEANUT BUTTER BROWNIES

Makes 24

- 1 (2-layer) package yellow cake mix
- 1 cup peanut butter
- 1/2 cup melted margarine
- 2 eggs
- 1 cup semisweet chocolate chips
- 1 1/3 cups sweetened condensed milk
- 2 tablespoons margarine
- 1 package coconut-pecan or coconut-almond frosting mix

Combine cake mix, peanut butter, melted margarine and eggs in bowl; mix to form dough. Press 2/3 of the mixture into ungreased 9x13-inch baking pan.

Combine chocolate chips, condensed milk and 2 tablespoons margarine in saucepan. Cook over low heat until chocolate and margarine are melted, stirring constantly; remove from heat. Stir in frosting mix. Spread in prepared pan. Crumble remaining dough over filling.

Bake at 350 degrees for 20 to 25 minutes or until golden brown. Cool in pan. Cut into bars.

Loleta Hammontree, Chattanooga, Tennessee

Camille is proud to say that her husband John and their two children, Patrick and Teresa, are alumni of UTK. "We love all sports and try to get to as many events as we can, whether football, basketball, baseball, track, or others. When Teresa was in school and working with the Lady Vols basketball program, I would try to bake them a few goodies. On one occasion, Daedra Charles proclaimed that she liked the chess squares, but, because they sort of stuck to the roof of your mouth, she called them 'Ooey-Gooeys.' From then on, that's how they were known. It really didn't hit home to me until the '93–'94 season, when someone saw me and asked if I had brought some Ooey-Gooeys!"

CHESS SQUARES (OOEY-GOOEYS)

Makes 24

1 (2-layer) package yellow cake mix
1/2 cup melted margarine
1 egg, beaten
1 (1-pound) package confectioners' sugar
2 eggs, beaten
8 ounces cream cheese, softened

Combine cake mix, margarine and 1 egg in bowl; mix well. Pat into 9x13-inch nonstick baking pan.

Combine confectioners' sugar, 2 eggs and cream cheese in bowl; mix well. Spread over cake mix mixture.

Bake at 325 degrees for 25 to 35 minutes or just until top is fluffy and brown around the edges. Chill thoroughly. Cut into squares.

You may wish to cut this very rich dessert into more than 24 portions. Do not use spreadable cream cheese in this recipe.

Camille G. Rotier, Hendersonville, Tennessee

COCOA CHIP COOKIES

Makes 72

2/3 cup shortening
1 1/2 cups sugar
2 eggs
2/3 cup sour cream
1 teaspoon vanilla extract
2 cups flour
1/2 cup baking cocoa
1/2 teaspoon baking soda
1/2 teaspoon salt
2 cups miniature chocolate chips

Cream shortening and sugar in mixer bowl until light and fluffy. Add eggs, sour cream and vanilla; beat well. Sift in flour, cocoa, baking soda and salt; mix well. Stir in chocolate chips. Drop by teaspoonfuls onto lightly greased cookie sheet.

Bake at 375 degrees for 8 to 10 minutes or until puffed and slightly cracked. Remove to wire rack to cool.

Janet E. Cordell, Dickson, Tennessee

**Janet, a graduate of the
College of Human Ecology, is
the Dickson County
Extension Leader for the
UT Agricultural Extension
Service, and these are a
favorite of 4-H Club
members in Dickson County.
She packs the cookies into
an airtight container to
keep them moist and chewy
for an after-game snack
in the parking lot on the
Ag campus.**

GINGERSNAPS

Makes 54

2 cups flour
1 teaspoon ginger
1 teaspoon cinnamon
2 teaspoons baking soda
1 teaspoon salt
3/4 cup shortening
1 cup sugar
1 egg
1/4 cup molasses
1/2 to 1 cup sugar

Sift flour, ginger, cinnamon, baking soda and salt together. Cream shortening and 1 cup sugar in mixer bowl until light and fluffy. Add egg and molasses; beat well. Add flour mixture gradually, beating well after each addition.

Shape by teaspoonfuls into small balls. Roll in remaining sugar. Place 2 inches apart on greased cookie sheet.

Bake at 350 degrees for 12 to 15 minutes or until browned.

■ This 25-year-old recipe won a prize at the county fair.

Susan Gould, Tennessee Ridge, Tennessee

MAGIC MOCHA DROPS

Makes 30

1/4 cup butter, softened
3/4 cup packed brown sugar
1 egg
1 1/3 cups baking mix
1 teaspoon instant coffee powder
1 (16-ounce) can chocolate frosting
30 pecan or walnut halves

Combine butter, brown sugar and egg in bowl; beat well. Stir in baking mix and coffee powder. Drop by teaspoonfuls onto ungreased cookie sheet.

Bake at 400 degrees for 8 to 10 minutes or until browned. Cool completely. Spread with frosting. Top with pecan halves.

■ This unusual recipe has been a favorite of friends for nearly 30 years. Coffee lovers will especially enjoy it at Big Orange tailgate parties!

Janet E. Cordell, Dickson, Tennessee

OATMEAL CHOCOLATE CHIP COOKIES

Makes 30

3/4 cup margarine, softened
1 cup packed light brown sugar
1/2 cup sugar
2 eggs
1 tablespoon water
1 teaspoon vanilla extract
1 teaspoon salt
1/2 teaspoon baking powder
1 cup sifted flour
1/2 cup wheat germ
2 1/2 cups quick-cooking oats
2 cups semisweet chocolate chips

Jenny Moshak became the Lady Vol Head Athletic Trainer in 1989.

Combine margarine, brown sugar, sugar, eggs, water, vanilla, salt and baking powder in mixer bowl; beat until smooth. Add flour, wheat germ and oats; mix well. Stir in chocolate chips. Drop by rounded tablespoonfuls onto cookie sheet sprayed with nonstick cooking spray.

Bake at 350 degrees for 12 to 15 minutes or until edges are golden brown. Remove to wire rack to cool.

You may add raisins, coconut and/or chopped walnuts to taste to batter.

■ These cookies taste best when served warm with a glass of cold milk. Caution: Although they are high in energy, these cookies should not be used to improve athletic performance!

Jennifer Moshak, Seymour, Tennessee

SKYBOX CUISINE

A FANCY SLICE

In the summer of 1994, Lamar Alexander, former President of the University of Tennessee, was invited to make the summer commencement address at Penn State. The night before, he visited with Joe Paterno, the Penn State coach, and reminded him that he had predicted that his Penn State team would be lucky to stay on the same field with Tennessee in the 1994 Citrus Bowl. Penn State won 31 to 13.

"It hasn't always been that way," Joe said. "We had a big problem with Tennessee in 1972. We had agreed to play a game, but not where to play it, and neither one of us wanted to back out because it would look like we were afraid to play it. So we met about it.

"Tennessee had Bob Woodruff for the Athletic Director. Woodruff could sit for six hours and not say a word. We started one morning at 4:00 A.M. and went until midnight and neither of us budged. Woodruff offered to make our game the opening game, but to play it in Knoxville. I wasn't about to go down to Knoxville for the opening game. It's much too hot then, but I didn't want to turn him down without a good reason. So after thinking for a while I finally said, 'Okay, we'll play it, but only if it's under the lights.' I knew they didn't have lights.

"It didn't take Woodruff ten seconds. 'You've got yourself a deal, Joe,' he said. That was in May, and in September UT had the lights up and they made a big thing out of it. It was the first Tennessee game under the lights. There was a capacity crowd there and they beat us. And we had a good team, too."

BAKED MUSHROOMS STUFFED WITH CRAB IMPERIAL

Makes 70

2 eggs
13/4 cups mayonnaise
1 tablespoon lemon juice
1/4 cup chopped parsley
1/2 teaspoon baking powder
1/4 teaspoon Worcestershire sauce
1/8 teaspoon cayenne pepper
2 teaspoons dry mustard
2 pounds Blue crab meat
70 large mushroom caps
11/2 cups fresh bread crumbs
1/2 cup melted butter

Combine eggs, mayonnaise, lemon juice, parsley, baking powder, Worcestershire sauce, cayenne pepper and dry mustard in bowl; whisk until well mixed.

Rinse and pick crab meat. Add to mayonnaise mixture; mix well. Spoon into mushroom caps; top with bread crumbs.

Place in baking dish. Add enough butter to cover bottom of baking dish.

Bake at 350 degrees for 12 to 15 minutes or until crab mixture reaches 165 degrees.

Paul Rentschler, Copper Cellar Restaurant, Knoxville, Tennessee

STUFFED MUSHROOMS

Serves 30

16 ounces fresh mushrooms
1 green onion, finely chopped
1/4 cup margarine
1 cup fresh bread crumbs
10 ounces fresh or frozen crab meat
1 tablespoon catsup
1 tablespoon lemon juice
1/4 teaspoon salt
Pepper to taste
15 slices bacon, cut into quarters
1/2 cup whipping cream

Remove and chop mushroom stems; set caps aside. Sauté chopped stems with green onion in margarine in 8-inch skillet. Stir in bread crumbs, crab meat, catsup, lemon juice, salt and pepper. Cook for 3 minutes or until heated through.

Spoon into mushroom caps; top each with crossed pieces of bacon, securing with wooden picks. Place in baking dish; pour cream around mushrooms.

Bake at 400 degrees for 20 minutes. Serve warm.

Joyce Willoughby, Gallatin, Tennessee

FESTIVE CHEESE MOLD

Serves 24

16 ounces sharp Cheddar cheese, shredded
1 1/2 cups chopped pecans
1 onion, finely chopped or grated
1 clove of garlic, minced
1 cup mayonnaise
1 teaspoon seasoned salt
1 cup hot pepper jelly or strawberry preserves

Mix cheese, pecans, onion, garlic, mayonnaise and seasoned salt in bowl. Shape into a ring or a roll on serving plate.

Chill until serving time. Spoon jelly into center or over top. Serve with crackers.

Becky Hedrick Kent, Nashville, Tennessee

SHRIMP AND CHEESE PATE

Serves 16

8 ounces cooked cleaned shrimp
2 envelopes unflavored gelatin
3/4 cup cold water
1/4 teaspoon salt
1 1/2 cups cottage cheese
3/4 cup chili sauce
1/2 cup sour cream
1/2 cup chopped celery (optional)

Cut 4 shrimp into halves lengthwise and set aside; chop remaining shrimp. Soften gelatin in cold water in saucepan. Add salt. Cook over low heat until gelatin dissolves. Add chopped shrimp, cottage cheese, chili sauce, sour cream and celery; mix well.

Arrange shrimp halves around side of lightly oiled 4-cup mold; fill mold with gelatin mixture. Chill until firm. Unmold onto lettuce-lined serving plate. Serve with crisp vegetables.

Melissa Arnold (1986), Bruceton, Tennessee

Becky Kent is the state consultant for home economics education, State Department of Education, and a graduate of the College of Human Ecology.

81

SEAFOOD FIESTA DIP

Serves 16

> 8 ounces cream cheese, softened
> 2 large avocados, cut into chunks
> 1 cup thick and chunky salsa
> 8 ounces imitation crab meat
> 1/3 cup black olives
> 1/4 cup sliced green onions with tops
> 2 ounces Cheddar cheese, shredded

Combine cream cheese and avocados in bowl; mix until smooth. Spread into 12-inch circle with rim on large serving plate. Spoon salsa evenly over circle.

Top with crab meat. Sprinkle with olives, green onions and Cheddar cheese. Chill for 2 hours. Serve with corn chips or crackers.

Sara Nichols, Nashville, Tennessee

The Nichols are such long-time Tennessee football fans that they can claim to have gone to a football game on their honeymoon in 1937. In that game on November 13, Tennessee played Vanderbilt and lost 13 to 7; each ticket cost $3.30. "We have had many wonderful experiences following the team in the years since then. Go Vols!"

SEAFOOD SOUP

Serves 8

- **1 large onion, chopped**
- **2 cloves of garlic, chopped**
- **1 large green bell pepper, chopped**
- **1/3 cup chopped parsley**
- **1/4 cup olive oil**
- **1 (28-ounce) can tomatoes**
- **1 (16-ounce) can tomato sauce**
- **1 cup red wine**
- **1 bay leaf**
- **1 teaspoon basil**
- **1/2 teaspoon oregano leaves**
- **1 pound uncooked shrimp, peeled**
- **1 pound crab meat**

Sauté onion, garlic, green pepper and parsley in olive oil in saucepan. Add tomatoes, tomato sauce, wine, bay leaf, basil and oregano; mix well. Bring to a boil and reduce heat. Simmer for 20 minutes.

Add shrimp and crab meat. Simmer, covered, just until the shrimp turn pink; discard bay leaf before serving.

You may also serve this over rice.

Joyce Mays, Gatlinburg, Tennessee

UT

The Mays have used this recipe for years on football Saturdays. "Our blood runs *deep* orange. My husband, Jack is a UT graduate and retired from the University in 1979; three of our children and one daughter-in-law also graduated from UT."

ELEGANT WILD RICE SOUP

Serves 6

 1 tablespoon minced onion
 6 tablespoons margarine
 1/3 cup flour
 3 cups chicken broth
 2 cups cooked wild rice
 1/2 cup finely grated carrot
 1/2 teaspoon salt
 1 cup half-and-half
 2 tablespoons sherry
 2 tablespoons chopped parsley

ᴜᴛ

Marian dedicates this wild rice soup recipe to her mentor and advisor at UT, Miss Ruth Buckley. "I still see some of the wonderful friends who made me welcome there as a transfer from Bradford Junior College in Massachusetts."

Sauté onion in margarine in saucepan until tender. Stir in flour. Add broth gradually. Bring to a boil. Cook for 1 minute or until thickened, stirring constantly.

Stir in rice, carrot and salt. Simmer for 5 to 10 minutes or until rice is tender. Add half-and-half and wine. Cook just until heated through. Garnish with parsley.

You may substitute low-fat milk for half-and-half if preferred and process in blender to thicken if necessary. For 2 cups cooked wild rice, cook 3/4 cup wild rice in 2 1/3 cups water.

Marian White Yarbro (1951), Jackson, Tennessee

SKYBOX CHILI

Serves 8

1 large onion, chopped
1 cup chopped celery
1 large green bell pepper, chopped
3 tablespoons olive oil
3 pounds extra-lean ground beef
1/2 cup packed brown sugar
1/2 cup wine vinegar
1/4 cup chili powder
1/2 teaspoon red pepper
1 (29-ounce) can tomatoes
2 (8-ounce) cans tomato sauce
2 bay leaves
1 tablespoon paprika
4 whole cloves
Salt to taste
2 (16-ounce) cans kidney beans, drained

Sauté onion, celery and green pepper in olive oil in heavy saucepan until tender. Add ground beef. Cook until ground beef is crumbly; drain. Add brown sugar, vinegar, chili powder and red pepper; reduce heat. Simmer for 15 minutes. Add tomatoes, tomato sauce, bay leaves, paprika, cloves and salt; mix well.

Spoon into slow cooker. Cook on Low for 4 hours, stirring occasionally. Add beans. Cook for 1 hour longer; discard bay leaves. Serve in warm bowls.

You may prepare this 1 day in advance in order to have it ready for before the game.

Ethel Bond Baker, Jackson, Tennessee

This old Baker family recipe has been used for many UT victory celebrations. "I have fond memories of playing on the freshman basketball team in 1928, long before the days of Pat Summitt. I lived in Barbara Blount Dormitory and when I could not attend a game, I'd watch it from my dormitory window—that was when the stadium was small, small. I am now 86 years old, and I still enjoy attending the games."

FRUITY CHICKEN SALAD

Serves 4

1 (8-ounce) can pineapple tidbits
1/4 cup mayonnaise
3 cups chopped cooked chicken
1 apple, chopped
1 1/2 cups seedless grape halves
1/2 cup slivered almonds
1/4 cup raisins (optional)

Drain pineapple, reserving 2 tablespoons juice. Combine reserved juice with mayonnaise in bowl; mix well. Add pineapple, chicken, apple, grapes, almonds and raisins; mix gently.

Chill for 1 hour or longer. Serve on lettuce leaves with crackers or as sandwich filling.

Representative Joe Kent, Memphis, Tennessee
District 83, Tennessee State House

NECTARINE BUFFET SALAD

Serves 10

1 cup vinegar
1/2 cup vegetable oil
1/2 cup sugar
4 nectarines, cut into wedges
4 tomatoes, cut into wedges
1 pound white mushrooms, cut into quarters
1 large sweet onion, sliced into rings, or 1 bunch green onions, diagonally sliced
2 green bell peppers, cut into 1-inch pieces
6 to 10 artichoke hearts, cut into halves

Combine vinegar, oil and sugar in large bowl; mix well. Add remaining ingredients; mix gently.

Marinate in refrigerator for 2 hours; drain. Arrange fruit and vegetables in serving bowl.

Ed and Carolyn Boling, Knoxville, Tennessee

UT

Edward J. Boling (1948, 1950) was president of the University of Tennessee from 1970 to 1988. He is a former Tennessee Commissioner of Finance and Administration. Carolyn Boling is a graduate of the College of Human Ecology and was awarded the Arch of Achievement Award by the college in 1990–91.

PASTA SALAD ROMA

Serves 8

8 ounces uncooked rotini
2 cups sliced mushrooms
2 (14-ounce) cans artichoke hearts, drained, quartered
2 cups cubed salami
2 cups cubed mozzarella cheese
1 cup sliced black olives
1 cup chopped red bell pepper
1/2 teaspoon seasoned salt
1/2 teaspoon freshly ground black pepper
2/3 cup olive oil
1/2 cup white wine vinegar
2 tablespoons Dijon mustard
1/2 cup chopped green onions
2 tablespoons minced parsley
3 cloves of garlic, crushed
1 teaspoon sugar
1 teaspoon dried basil leaves
1/2 teaspoon dried oregano leaves
1/2 teaspoon crushed red pepper flakes
1/2 teaspoon salt

Cook pasta using package directions; rinse with cold water and drain. Combine with mushrooms, artichoke hearts, salami, cheese, olives, bell pepper, seasoned salt and black pepper in large bowl.

Combine olive oil, vinegar, mustard, green onions, parsley, garlic, sugar, basil, oregano, red pepper flakes and salt in covered jar; shake to mix well. Add to pasta mixture; mix gently. Chill, tightly covered, for up to 3 days.

■ This is great for tailgating before and after the games at Neyland Stadium. Serve it with French bread and a glass of wine.

Mary Ann Harding, Germantown, Tennessee

TENNESSEE TORTELLINI SALAD

Serves 12

1/2 cup olive oil
1/4 cup white wine vinegar
1/4 cup chopped green onions
3 cloves of garlic, chopped
1 tablespoon basil, crumbled
1 teaspoon dillweed
1/2 teaspoon salt
2 (12-ounce) packages frozen cheese-stuffed tortellini
1 (8-ounce) can artichoke hearts, drained, quartered
1 large tomato, chopped
1/2 cup each crumbled feta cheese, chopped black olives
  and walnuts

Whisk olive oil and vinegar in small bowl. Add green onions, garlic, basil, dillweed and salt; mix well.

Cook pasta using package directions; drain. Combine with artichoke hearts, tomato, cheese, olives and walnuts in large bowl. Add dressing; mix gently. Chill for 8 hours or longer.

Missy Daniel (1977), Franklin, Tennessee

ZESTY PASTA SALAD

Serves 8

1 pound pasta, cooked
1 pound feta cheese, crumbled
1 tomato, chopped
1 green bell pepper, chopped
1 (16-ounce) can black olives, drained
1 (16-ounce) bottle zesty Italian salad dressing
1/4 cup grated Parmesan cheese

Combine pasta, feta cheese, tomato, green pepper and olives in large bowl; mix well. Add salad dressing and Parmesan cheese; mix gently. Chill until serving time. Serve cold.

Cynthia Slatton, Brentwood, Tennessee

ROASTED POTATO SALAD WITH GREEN BEANS AND RED ONION

Serves 10

- 3 pounds red boiling potatoes
- 1/3 cup olive oil
- 1 clove of garlic
- 1/4 cup red wine vinegar
- 1 tablespoon fresh rosemary or 1 teaspoon dried
- Salt to taste
- 1/3 cup olive oil
- 2 pounds green beans, cut into 1-inch pieces
- 1 red onion
- 30 kalamata or niçoise olives, cut into halves

Cut unpeeled potatoes into halves and then into 1-inch wedges. Combine with 1/3 cup olive oil in large roasting pan, tossing to coat well. Roast at 450 degrees for 30 minutes or until tender, stirring every 10 minutes. Cool potatoes in pan.

Process garlic, vinegar, rosemary, salt and 1/3 cup olive oil in blender until smooth.

Cook beans in salted water in saucepan for 5 minutes or until tender-crisp; drain. Cut onion into halves lengthwise and then into thin slices. Crisp in ice water in bowl for 5 minutes; drain and pat dry.

Combine potatoes, beans, onion, olives and dressing in bowl; toss lightly to coat well. Garnish with sprigs of fresh rosemary. Serve at room temperature.

■ We find this to be a terrific salad for early fall tailgate parties.

Honey and Lamar Alexander, Nashville, Tennessee

Lamar Alexander was Governor of Tennessee from 1979 to 1986. He served as the 18th president of the University of Tennessee from 1988 to 1991. In March of 1991, he left the University to become the United States Secretary of Education.

BLEU CHEESE POTATO SALAD

Serves 10

8 medium potatoes, peeled, chopped
3 green onions with tops, chopped
1/2 cup toasted slivered almonds
3 hard-cooked eggs, chopped
2 tablespoons chopped parsley
4 ounces bleu cheese, crumbled
1 cup sour cream
1/4 cup white wine vinegar
2 1/2 teaspoons salt
1/4 teaspoon white pepper

Cook potatoes in water in saucepan until tender; drain. Combine with green onions, almonds, eggs, parsley and bleu cheese in bowl; mix well.

Add sour cream, vinegar, salt and white pepper; mix gently.

You may add crumbled crisp-fried bacon if desired.

Dottie McKinney, Knoxville, Tennessee

HALF-TIME BEEF SANDWICHES

Serves 6

- 1 small apple, finely chopped
- 2 teaspoons lemon juice
- 3 ounces cream cheese, softened
- 1 tablespoon milk
- 1 tablespoon prepared horseradish
- 1/3 cup walnut pieces
- 6 Kaiser rolls, split
- 1 pound thickly sliced deli roast beef
- 6 lettuce leaves
- 2 tablespoons sliced green onions

Sprinkle apple with lemon juice. Mix cream cheese, milk and undrained horseradish in bowl. Add apple and walnuts; mix well.

Spread mixture over cut sides of rolls. Place beef, lettuce and green onions on bottom halves of rolls; replace tops. Serve immediately or wrap in plastic wrap and chill for up to 4 hours.

Wanda Brown, Hermitage, Tennessee
Bettye Erb, Old Hickory, Tennessee
Submitted by Dean Don Richardson
Agricultural Extension Station, Knoxville

THE BAMA SURPRISE

Serves 4

- 3 tablespoons olive oil
- 4 (8-ounce) fillet steaks
- 16 ounces mushrooms, sliced
- 2 cloves of garlic, chopped
- 1 cup marsala

Heat olive oil in 14-inch skillet over medium-high heat. Add steaks. Cook until brown on both sides. Add mushrooms and garlic; cook until mushrooms are tender. Add wine. Cook until steaks are done to taste. Serve with pasta.

Jessee Meade, Ocean City, Maryland

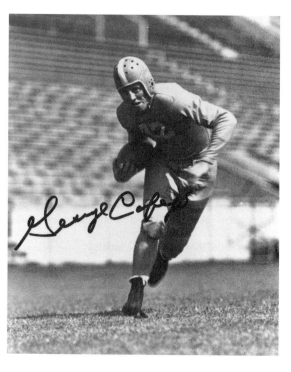

HUNGARIAN CABBAGE ROLLS

Serves 6

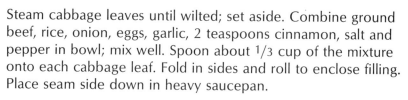

George Cafego was a Vol tailback and All-America in 1938 and 1939. He played for the Brooklyn Dodgers, the Washington Redskins and the Boston Yanks from 1940 through 1944. He is a member of the College Football Hall of Fame. He was on the Pre-1940 team selected during the "100 Years of Volunteers" celebration in 1990. An assistant coach from 1963 to 1984, he developed many of the Vols' finest kickers. His most memorable experience at UT, however, was in 1936, when "I stepped off the bus, a scared 146-pound young man, and realized that I might get the chance to become a Tennessee Volunteer and play in that huge stadium that seated 35,000."

6 outer cabbage leaves
2 pounds ground beef
1 cup cooked rice
1 large onion, chopped
2 eggs
1 clove of garlic, minced
2 teaspoons cinnamon
1 teaspoon salt
1/2 teaspoon pepper
1 (16-ounce) can tomato sauce
4 teaspoons brown sugar
1/4 cup water
1 tablespoon lemon juice
Cinnamon to taste

Steam cabbage leaves until wilted; set aside. Combine ground beef, rice, onion, eggs, garlic, 2 teaspoons cinnamon, salt and pepper in bowl; mix well. Spoon about 1/3 cup of the mixture onto each cabbage leaf. Fold in sides and roll to enclose filling. Place seam side down in heavy saucepan.

Combine tomato sauce, brown sugar, water and lemon juice in bowl; mix well. Pour over cabbage rolls; sprinkle with additional cinnamon. Cook, covered, over low heat for 1 hour, spooning sauce over rolls occasionally.

George Cafego, Knoxville, Tennessee

LASAGNA WITH FOUR CHEESES

Serves 6

    6 uncooked lasagna noodles
    4 ounces cream cheese, softened
    8 ounces small curd cottage cheese, drained
    8 ounces sour cream
    1/4 cup finely chopped onion
    11/2 pounds ground chuck
    1/2 large onion, chopped
    1 (8-ounce) can tomato sauce
    1 (16-ounce) jar spaghetti sauce
    1 envelope spaghetti sauce mix
    1/2 teaspoon sugar
    1/4 teaspoon garlic powder
    1/2 cup shredded Cheddar cheese
    1/2 cup shredded mozzarella cheese

Cook noodles using package directions; place in cold water until needed. Mix cream cheese, cottage cheese, sour cream and 1/4 cup onion in bowl.

Brown ground beef with 1/2 chopped onion in saucepan, stirring until ground beef is crumbly; drain. Add tomato sauce, spaghetti sauce, spaghetti sauce mix, sugar and garlic powder. Simmer for 15 minutes or longer, stirring occasionally.

Layer noodles, meat sauce and cottage cheese mixture 1/2 at a time in 9x13-inch baking dish. Top with Cheddar cheese and mozzarella cheese.

Bake at 350 degrees for 35 to 45 minutes or until bubbly. Let stand for 15 minutes before serving.

You may freeze the lasagna and thaw it in the refrigerator before baking.

Deborah D. Canter, Ph.D., R.D., Manhattan, Kansas

Deborah (1974) says, "this recipe is the result of experimentation while I was a graduate student in the College of Human Ecology at UT and has long been a favorite of family and friends."

Condredge played quarterback on Tennessee teams from 1972 to 1974, earning the nickname of the "Artful Dodger" for his ability to scramble out of danger. He was the first black quarterback in the SEC and led the team in offense in each of his three varsity years; he is fifth on the all-time Tennessee total offense list with 4068 yards total offense.

CHICKEN COURTNEY

Serves 2

2 chicken breasts, skinned
Olive oil
Honey
Char-seasoning

Wash chicken and pat dry. Rub with olive oil, honey and char-seasoning. Marinate in refrigerator for 1 hour or longer.

Grill chicken until tender and cooked through.

■ This recipe was an experiment and rest is history!

Condredge Holloway, Knoxville, Tennessee

SEAFOOD DELIGHT

Serves 6

> 2 (16-ounce) cans asparagus spears, drained
> 8 ounces Cheddar cheese, shredded
> 1 (7-ounce) can lobster meat, drained
> 1 (7-ounce) can crab meat, drained
> 1 (7-ounce) can shrimp
> 3 (4-ounce) cans sliced mushrooms, drained
> 2 (10-ounce) cans cream of mushroom soup
> 1/2 cup almonds
> 1/2 cup bread crumbs

Layer asparagus, 1/3 of the cheese, lobster, crab meat, shrimp, 1/3 of the cheese and mushrooms in buttered baking dish. Spread soup over layers. Top with almonds, bread crumbs and remaining cheese.

Bake at 350 degrees for 40 minutes.

Jim and Natalie Haslam
Knoxville, Tennessee

Natalie and Jim are both graduates of the University. Jim was the captain of the UT football team in 1952 and is now CEO of Pilot Oil Company. He is a several-term member of the UT Board of Trustees, serving on the development, health affairs, and finance committees. He has served as vice-chairman of the Board of Trustees. The Haslams are both leaders in the Knoxville community and are strong supporters of UT.

BATTERED FRIED SHRIMP

Serves 6

> 1 egg
> 1 cup milk
> 1 1/2 cups flour
> 1 tablespoon baking powder
> 1/4 teaspoon salt
> 2 pounds peeled shrimp
> Vegetable oil for frying

Beat egg in bowl. Add milk and beat until smooth. Sift in flour, baking powder and salt; mix well. Dip shrimp into batter, coating well.

Fry shrimp in 375-degree oil in saucepan for 2 to 3 minutes or until golden brown; drain well.

Stanley and Rholedia Morgan, Germantown, Tennessee

Stanley Morgan played wide receiver and tailback at the University from 1973 to 1976, earning All-SEC honors in 1974 and 1976. He was a first-round draft choice of the New England Patriots and later played for the Indianapolis Colts. He is sixth on the Tennessee all-time rushing list with 1952 yards over his career. He had 201 yards rushing against Hawaii in 1975, a record which stood for nine years. Rholedia has her own business in the Memphis area and is a graduate of the College of Human Ecology.

STAR-SPANGLED BAKED SHRIMP

Serves 6

- 2 medium onions, finely chopped
- 3 cloves of garlic, minced
- 6 tablespoons olive oil
- 2 (14-ounce) cans tomatoes with green chiles
- 2 (14-ounce) cans crushed tomatoes
- 1/4 teaspoon sugar
- Salt to taste
- 2 pounds shrimp, peeled, deveined
- 3 tablespoons butter or olive oil
- 2 tablespoons olive oil
- 6 tablespoons ouzo
- 6 tablespoons Cognac
- 8 ounces feta cheese, crumbled
- 1/4 cup chopped fresh parsley

Sauté onions and garlic lightly in 6 tablespoons heated olive oil in heavy saucepan. Squeeze tomatoes into small pieces. Add to saucepan with sugar and salt; mix well. Cook over medium heat until thickened to desired consistency.

Sauté shrimp in butter and 2 tablespoons olive oil in large heavy skillet over medium-high heat until pink. Add ouzo and Cognac. Ignite mixture and let flames subside.

Spoon shrimp into baking dish or ramekins. Top with tomato sauce; sprinkle with cheese and parsley.

Bake at 425 degrees for 10 to 15 minutes or until shrimp is bubbly and cheese melts. Serve with crusty bread and salad.

George Bitzas, Knoxville, Tennessee

George Bitzas is a professor in the Department of Music at the University. He is best known by Vol fans for his stirring rendition of the "Star-Spangled Banner" at UT home football games.

SEAFOOD CASSEROLE

Serves 6

1/4 cup flour
1/4 cup melted butter
2 cups milk
8 ounces sharp Cheddar cheese, shredded
1/2 teaspoon dry mustard
1 tablespoon chopped parsley
2 tablespoons minced onion
1 (4-ounce) can crab meat, drained
1 (14-ounce) package frozen shrimp, thawed, drained
1 (8-ounce) can sliced mushrooms, drained
2 tablespoons bread crumbs
1 teaspoon butter
Paprika to taste

Blend flour into melted butter in saucepan. Cook until bubbly; remove from heat. Stir in milk. Cook for 10 minutes or until thickened, stirring constantly; remove from heat. Stir in cheese, dry mustard, parsley and onion.

Add crab meat, shrimp and mushrooms to cheese sauce. Spoon into 2-quart baking dish. Brown bread crumbs in 1 teaspoon butter in skillet. Sprinkle over casserole; top with paprika.

Bake at 350 degrees for 25 to 30 minutes or until bubbly and heated through.

Eli and Cathy Fly, Knoxville, Tennessee

Emerson H. Fly (1961) became the Executive Vice President of the University in 1991, and has been the Vice President for Business and Finance since 1976.

ASPARAGUS CASSEROLE

Serves 4

1 tablespoon flour
1/2 teaspoon seasoned salt
1 tablespoon melted butter or margarine
1/2 cup milk
1/2 cup shredded Swiss cheese
1 (14-ounce) can asparagus
1 cup French-fried onions

Blend flour and seasoned salt into melted butter in saucepan. Add milk gradually. Cook over low heat until thickened, stirring constantly. Stir in cheese until melted.

Heat undrained asparagus in saucepan; drain. Add to sauce with half the onions; mix gently. Spoon into baking dish; top with remaining onions.

Bake at 350 degrees until bubbly.

Leslie Dickey, Nashville, Tennessee

Leslie Dickey is Vol baseball pitcher R.A. Dickey's mother. She describes his eating habits in this way: "I'm afraid R.A.'s taste buds were quite limited growing up. At age five, his favorite foods were Trix cereal and Kraft Macaroni and Cheese. At age nine, his favorite foods were Trix cereal and Kraft Macaroni and Cheese. At age fifteen, his favorite foods were Lucky Charms cereal and Kraft Macaroni and Cheese. Now, at age twenty, his favorite foods are cornflakes with bananas and Velveeta Shells and Cheese. As you can see, he has acquired *some* variety. However, I did manage to get him to eat a few green things; Asparagus Casserole (believe it or not) is still one of his favorites."

BROCCOLI-STUFFED TOMATOES

Serves 8

8 medium tomatoes
Salt and pepper to taste
1 (10-ounce) package frozen chopped broccoli
1 cup shredded Swiss cheese
1 cup soft bread crumbs
1/2 cup mayonnaise
2 tablespoons chopped green onions
1/4 teaspoon garlic powder
1/4 teaspoon cayenne pepper
3/4 cup grated Parmesan cheese

Cut tops from tomatoes. Remove and discard pulp and seeds from tomatoes, reserving shells. Sprinkle shells with salt and pepper; invert onto rack to drain for 30 minutes or longer.

Cook broccoli using package directions; drain. Combine with Swiss cheese, bread crumbs, mayonnaise, green onions, garlic powder, cayenne pepper and 1/2 cup of the Parmesan cheese in bowl; mix well.

Stuff broccoli mixture into tomato shells. Place in baking dish; sprinkle with remaining 1/4 cup Parmesan cheese.

Bake at 350 degrees for 25 minutes.

You may prepare this in advance and chill, covered, for up to 24 hours.

Mary A. McAllester (1975), Nashville, Tennessee

Mary is the grandaughter of Sam J. McAllester, who played football for UT in 1903 and 1904.

FRESH MUSHROOM CASSEROLE

Serves 8

1 1/2 pounds fresh mushrooms, sliced
1/2 cup chopped onion
1/4 cup vegetable oil
Garlic salt to taste
1/2 cup mayonnaise
2 eggs, beaten
1 (10-ounce) can cream of mushroom soup
1 1/2 cups milk
3 cups shredded Cheddar cheese
3/4 teaspoon salt
8 to 10 slices white bread

Sauté mushrooms and onion in oil in skillet until tender but not brown. Add garlic salt. Combine mayonnaise, eggs, soup, milk, cheese and salt in bowl; mix well. Add mushroom mixture; mix well.

Trim crusts from bread; cut bread slices into cubes. Press 2/3 of the bread cubes over bottom and side of greased 2-quart baking dish. Layer half the mushroom mixture, remaining bread cubes and remaining mushroom mixture in prepared dish.

Chill, covered, for 8 hours or longer. Let stand at room temperature for 45 to 60 minutes before baking.

Bake at 325 degrees for 30 to 40 minutes or until bubbly and golden brown.

Mary Jo Baldwin Dougherty (1952), Camden, Tennessee

Mary Jo is a graduate of the College of Human Ecology and is a former Women's Council Member. Her husband Lew was president of the National Alumni Association in 1982–1983.

RATATOUILLE

Serves 16

Betty, a 1953 graduate of UT, is the wife of Hank Lauricella, All-America tailback at Tennessee in the 1951 national championship season and runner-up for the Heisman Trophy that same year. He is a member of the College Football Hall of Fame and the Louisiana State Senate.

2 (8-ounce) eggplant
1 pound zucchini
2 teaspoons salt
1/2 cup olive oil
2 pounds onions, thinly sliced
4 green bell peppers, sliced
4 cloves of garlic, minced
2 pounds tomatoes, peeled and chopped, or
   1 (32-ounce) can Italian tomatoes
1/4 teaspoon thyme
1 bunch fresh basil
Minced parsley to taste
Salt and pepper to taste
1 tablespoon tomato paste

General Bob Neyland,
Coach of Tennessee
1926–1934, 1936–1940, 1946–1952,
with Hank Lauricella

Cut unpeeled eggplant and zucchini into cubes. Toss with 2 teaspoons salt in bowl. Let stand for 30 minutes; drain and pat dry.

Sauté eggplant and zucchini in olive oil in skillet until light brown. Add onions and green peppers. Sauté for 10 minutes. Reserve 1 teaspoon of the garlic. Stir in remaining garlic, tomatoes, thyme, basil, parsley and salt and pepper to taste. Cook, covered, for 15 to 20 minutes or until vegetables are tender, stirring frequently.

Add tomato paste. Simmer, covered, for 10 minutes. Adjust seasonings and add reserved garlic and additional parsley. Simmer for 15 minutes longer. Serve hot or cold. Flavor improves after chilling for two or three days.

Hank and Betty Lauricella

ROLLS FOR "HAM BISCUITS"

Makes 70

- 2 envelopes dry yeast
- 1 cup lukewarm water
- 1 cup shortening
- 3/4 cup sugar
- 1 cup boiling water
- 2 eggs
- 7 to 8 cups flour
- 1 teaspoon salt

Dissolve yeast in lukewarm water. Cream shortening and sugar in mixer bowl until light and fluffy. Add boiling water; stir until dissolved; cool slightly. Add eggs and yeast; mix well.

Combine flour and salt. Sift half the flour and salt into the creamed mixture. Add enough remaining flour mixture to form an easily-handled dough. Place in buttered bowl, turning to coat surface. Let rise in refrigerator for 8 hours or until doubled in bulk.

Roll on floured surface and cut into 2-inch circles. Place on greased baking sheet. Let rise in warm place for 2 hours or until doubled in bulk.

Bake at 350 to 375 degrees for 8 to 10 minutes or until golden brown. Cool on wire racks and store in sealable plastic bags.

Martha Chase Holt, Knoxville, Tennessee

Dr. Andy Holt was President of the University of Tennessee from 1959 to 1970. He is recognized as one of America's leading educators and has been awarded many national and regional honors. Martha tells us that during their years in the presidency, "we made these rolls for ham biscuits on occasions for faculty, students and friends of the university. He thought country ham biscuits the very best item that could be served for a tea or casual supper. Most of the time he sliced the ham and broiled it himself so it would be perfect! These are better than biscuits because they don't crumble on the carpet."

FRESH APPLE CAKE

Serves 16

1¹/2 cups vegetable oil
3 eggs
2 cups sugar
3 cups flour
1 teaspoon baking soda
1 teaspoon salt
2 teaspoons vanilla extract
3 large apples, chopped
1 cup chopped pecans
¹/2 cup margarine
2 tablespoons milk
¹/2 cup packed brown sugar

Combine oil, eggs and sugar in mixer bowl; beat at medium speed for 3 minutes. Add flour, baking soda, salt and vanilla; mix well. Fold in apples and pecans. Spoon into greased and floured tube pan.

Bake at 350 degrees for 1 hour and 20 minutes. Cool in pan for 20 minutes. Remove to serving plate.

Combine margarine, milk and brown sugar in saucepan. Bring to a boil and cook for 2 minutes. Pour hot sauce over cake.

■ You may freeze this cake. Leave off the sauce for a wonderful take-along cake for tailgating.

Muriel F. Bradley (1944), Savannah, Tennessee

MOCHA BROWNIE TORTE CAKE

Serves 12

- **1 family-size package brownie mix**
- **1 cup chocolate chips**
- **1 tablespoon instant coffee**
- **1 tablespoon boiling water**
- **1 1/2 cups whipping cream**
- **1/3 cup packed brown sugar**

Kevin O'Neill became UT's 14th head basketball coach in March of 1994, following a five-year position at Marquette. At age 37, he was the youngest coach in the Southeastern Conference.

Prepare brownie mix, adding chocolate chips. Bake in two 9x9-inch baking pans for 10 minutes or use package directions. Cool in pans for 5 minutes; remove to wire rack to cool completely.

Dissolve coffee in boiling water. Cool to room temperature. Whip cream in mixer bowl until frothy. Add brown sugar and coffee mixture, beating until soft peaks form. Spread between layers and over top of torte. Chill for 4 to 8 hours. Garnish with chocolate curls.

■ This can be made in advance, so when we plan a party after the game, it is ready.

Kevin and Martha O'Neill, Knoxville, Tennessee

BLUE RIBBON CARROT CAKE

Serves 16

3 eggs, beaten
3/4 cup vegetable oil
3/4 cup buttermilk
2 cups sugar
2 teaspoons vanilla extract
2 cups flour
2 teaspoons baking soda
2 teaspoons cinnamon
1/2 teaspoon salt
1 (8-ounce) can crushed pineapple, drained
2 cups grated carrots
1 cup flaked coconut
1 cup chopped walnuts or pecans
Buttermilk Glaze
Orange Cream Cheese Frosting

Combine eggs, oil, buttermilk, sugar and vanilla in bowl; beat until smooth. Combine flour, baking soda, cinnamon and salt. Add to egg mixture with pineapple, carrots, coconut and walnuts; mix well. Spoon into 2 greased and floured 9-inch cake pans.

Bake at 350 degrees for 35 to 40 minutes or until cake tester comes out clean. Spread Buttermilk Glaze over layers immediately. Cool in pans for 15 minutes. Remove to wire rack to cool completely.

Spread Orange Cream Cheese Frosting between layers and over top and side of cake. Store in refrigerator.

(continued)

Buttermilk Glaze

1/2 cup buttermilk
1 tablespoon light corn syrup
1/2 cup butter
1 cup sugar
1/2 teaspoon baking soda
1 teaspoon vanilla extract

Combine buttermilk, corn syrup, butter, sugar and baking soda in saucepan. Bring to a boil. Cook for 4 minutes, stirring frequently; remove from heat. Stir in vanilla.

Orange Cream Cheese Frosting

1/2 cup butter, softened
8 ounces cream cheese, softened
2 cups sifted confectioners' sugar
1 teaspoon orange juice
1 teaspoon grated orange rind
1 teaspoon vanilla extract

Beat butter and cream cheese in mixer bowl until light. Add confectioners' sugar, orange juice, orange rind and vanilla; beat until smooth.

Armistine Shepherd, Knoxville, Tennessee

Allan Houston

Henrietta Harper, a retired Home Economics teacher, is Allan Houston's aunt. She says that Congo Bars are one of his favorites. Allan, who played basketball at UT from 1990 to 1993, is the University's all-time scorer, with 2801 points. He was a first-round draft choice of the Detroit Pistons in 1993. He is the son of former Vol basketball coach Wade Houston.

CONGO BARS

Makes 28

> 2/3 cup shortening
> 1 (1-pound) package brown sugar
> 3 eggs
> 2 3/4 cups sifted flour
> 2 1/2 teaspoons baking powder
> 1/2 teaspoon salt
> 1 cup chopped pecans
> 1 cup semisweet chocolate chips

Melt shortening and brown sugar in saucepan over low heat, stirring to mix well. Cool slightly. Beat in eggs 1 at a time.

Sift in flour, baking powder and salt; mix well. Stir in pecans and chocolate chips. Spoon into greased 10x14-inch baking pan.

Bake at 350 degrees for 25 to 30 minutes. Cool on wire rack. Cut into bars.

Henrietta Harper, Knoxville, Tennessee

FILLED CANNOLI

Serves 15

> 1 1/2 pounds ricotta cheese
> 1 cup confectioners' sugar
> 1 tablespoon vanilla extract
> 2 ounces bittersweet chocolate, grated
> 4 ounces toasted almonds
> 30 (4-inch) cannoli shells

Pulse half the ricotta cheese in food processor until smooth; transfer to bowl. Pulse remaining ricotta cheese with confectioners' sugar and vanilla. Add to bowl; mix well. Fold in chocolate and almonds.

Spoon into pastry bag fitted with regular tip. Pipe into cannoli shells. Garnish with additional confectioners' sugar

Italian Market and Grill, Knoxville, Tennessee

STRAWBERRY DELIGHT

Serves 15

1/4 cup packed brown sugar
1 cup flour
1/2 cup chopped pecans
1/2 cup butter
1 (10-ounce) package frozen strawberries, thawed
2 egg whites
1 cup sugar
1 tablespoon lemon juice
1 teaspoon vanilla extract
16 ounces whipped topping

Mix brown sugar, flour, pecans and butter in bowl until crumbly. Spread in greased 9x13-inch baking dish. Bake at 400 degrees for 15 minutes or until golden brown, stirring occasionally. Reserve half the crumb mixture; spread remaining crumbs evenly in dish.

Combine strawberries, egg whites, sugar, lemon juice and vanilla in mixer bowl; beat at high speed for 15 to 20 minutes or until very stiff. Fold in whipped topping.

Spoon into prepared dish; sprinkle with reserved crumbs. Freeze for 8 hours or longer. Cut into squares to serve.

Carolyn Jo Harris, Knoxville, Tennessee

Carolyn Jo is the wife of Haywood Harris. Haywood became Associate Athletic Director for Media Relations in 1989 after serving for 26 years as Sports Information Director and three years as Assistant Athletic Director. Considered an authority on Tennessee athletics, he is in charge of media relations for Athletic Director Doug Dickey, football coach Phillip Fulmer, and basketball coach Kevin O'Neill; he is also in charge of overseeing the operations of the Sports Information Office.

ROCKY TOP PEANUT BUTTER PIE

Serves 6

1/2 cup peanut butter
1 cup confectioners' sugar
1 baked pie shell
2 cups milk
2/3 cup sugar
1/4 cup cornstarch or 1/2 cup flour
1/4 teaspoon salt
3 egg yolks, beaten
2 tablespoons butter or margarine
1/2 teaspoon vanilla extract
3 egg whites
1/4 cup sugar

Rocky Top Peanut Butter Pie is a favorite of Nana DeWitt's (Ruth Johnston DeWitt's) Vol sons, grandchildren and great-grandchildren. An avid fan herself, she always watches the games on the television—unless she gets upset with the score, at which time she turns off the set and reads about the game in the paper the next day.

Combine peanut butter and confectioners' sugar in bowl; mix until crumbly. Reserve 1/3 of the mixture. Spread remaining mixture in pie shell.

Scald milk in double boiler. Add mixture of 2/3 cup sugar, cornstarch and salt; mix well. Stir in egg yolks. Cook until thickened, stirring constantly. Stir in butter and vanilla. Cool to room temperature. Pour into pie shell.

Beat egg whites until soft peaks form. Add 1/4 cup sugar, beating constantly until stiff peaks form. Spread over pie, sealing to edge. Sprinkle with reserved peanut butter mixture.

Bake at 350 degrees just until meringue is light brown.

Barbara DeWitt Johnson, Greeneville, Tennessee

A SEA OF ORANGE

The allegiance of many UT football fans goes back a very long way. The McAllester football tradition goes back to 1903 and 1904, when Sam J. McAllester played fullback for UT. His most outstanding accomplishment was scoring the only and winning touchdown against Alabama on November 24, 1904. As he told it, before the game the coach had developed a large leather belt with a handle on either side. In the touchdown drive, Sam ran toward the line of scrimmage and the two halfbacks grabbed the handles and threw him across the line of scrimmage for the winning score.

By comparison, Jimmy Hahn was a relative newcomer to UT football. He played blocking back at Tennessee from 1948 to 1951. His memories of those days are still vivid: "When I tried out for the Tennessee football team in the spring of 1948, General Robert Neyland told me that I would be a blocking back—'the most important position on the team,' he said. It sounded good to me. Then he said that I would play on a National Championship Team. That I found harder to believe. General Neyland was right! After starting each varsity game throughout the '49 to '51 seasons, I played quarterback on the 1951 National Championship Team my senior year, and the same year was awarded the Jacobs Blocking trophy as best blocker in the SEC.

BIG ORANGE SHRIMP MOLD

Serves 6

2 envelopes unflavored gelatin
1/4 cup cold water
1 (10-ounce) can tomato soup
8 ounces cream cheese, softened
3/4 cup mayonnaise
1/4 cup sandwich spread
1 bunch green onions, chopped
1 cup chopped celery
2 to 3 pounds chopped cooked shrimp or 2 pounds cooked
   popcorn shrimp
1 teaspoon salt
1 teaspoon red pepper flakes
1/4 teaspoon garlic powder

Soften gelatin in water in large bowl. Warm soup by running hot water over can for 5 minutes; do not heat on stove. Add soup to gelatin; mix well. Beat in cream cheese until smooth. Add mayonnaise and sandwich spread; mix well. Stir in green onions, celery and shrimp. Stir in salt, red pepper and garlic powder.

Pour mixture into mold and chill for 8 hours. Serve with butter crackers.

■ This mold is a favorite at tailgate parties or during post-game celebrations.

Bobby Fischer, Knoxville, Tennessee

The Big Orange Shrimp Mold has been in Bobby Fischer's family for years—he and his wife have served it before and during games in every state where they have lived, including Louisiana, Florida, Arizona and Texas. The mold has convinced people across the country to become UT fans.

BIG ORANGE PUNCH

Serves 20

> 2 small packages sugar-free orange gelatin
> 2 1/2 cups sugar or 8 tablespoons sugar substitute
> 2 cups boiling water
> 2 cups cold water
> 2 (12-ounce) cans frozen lemonade concentrate
> 2 (46-ounce) cans pineapple juice
> 2 (1-liter) bottles ginger ale

Dissolve gelatin and sugar in boiling water in bowl. Add cold water, lemonade concentrate and pineapple juice; mix well. Pour into 1/2- or 1-gallon containers.

Freeze for 8 hours. Combine 1 liter ginger ale with each 1/2 gallon frozen liquid in punch bowl; mix gently.

Lois Faye Batten, Lewisburg, Tennessee
Trish Dorsey, Brentwood, Tennessee

UT

Trish is a 1968 graduate of UT. She is the wife of Al Dorsey, who played football at UT from 1965 to 1967. She and her husband served Big Orange Punch at their home for several years to prospective scholarship recipients and their parents, with whom it was very popular.

ORANGE NECTAR PUNCH

Serves 60

> 2 (6-ounce) envelopes orange drink mix
> 2 (46-ounce) cans pineapple juice
> 2 (46-ounce) cans orange juice
> 1 (46-ounce) can apricot nectar
> 1 (12-ounce) can apricot nectar
> 1 cup sugar
> 1 cup (about) boiling water
> Juice of 6 lemons

Mix orange drink mix, pineapple juice, orange juice and apricot nectar in large container. Dissolve sugar in boiling water and lemon juice; mix well. Add to juice mixture.

Pour about 1/3 of the mixture into ice trays. Freeze until firm. Chill remaining punch. Combine with frozen punch in bowl.

Brenda Loyd, Johnson City, Tennessee

BIG ORANGE SLUSHEE PUNCH

Serves 30

2 small oranges, sliced, seeded
1 (6-ounce) jar maraschino cherries, drained
1 (34-ounce) bottle ginger ale
1 (12-ounce) can frozen orange juice concentrate, diluted
1 (46-ounce) can pineapple juice
1/4 cup lime juice
3/4 cup sugar
1 (28-ounce) bottle tonic water, chilled
2 (34-ounce) bottles ginger ale, chilled

Cut orange slices in half. Line bottom of 6¹/2-cup ring mold with half the orange slices and cherries. Pour in thin layer of unchilled ginger ale and freeze until firm.

Arrange remaining orange slices and cherries along the sides of ring mold and pour in another thin layer of unchilled ginger ale. Freeze until firm. Add remaining unchilled ginger ale. Freeze until firm.

Combine orange juice, pineapple juice, lime juice and sugar in large container, stirring until sugar dissolves. Chill until ready to serve. Pour juice mixture into punch bowl at serving time. Add tonic water, remaining ginger ale and ice ring.

Kim Middlebrooks, Knoxville, Tennessee

ORANGE JULIUS

Serves 2

1 (6-ounce) can frozen orange juice concentrate
1/2 cup sugar or to taste
1/2 cup milk
1/2 cup water
1/2 teaspoon vanilla extract

Combine orange juice, sugar, milk, water and vanilla in blender container; process until smooth. Chill until serving time.

Brenda Loyd, Johnson City, Tennessee

115

ORANGE CRUSH SODA

Serves 1

1 tablespoon orange liqueur
1 (12-ounce) can orange soda
2 large scoops vanilla ice cream or orange sorbet
Seltzer or club soda (optional)

Combine the orange liqueur with enough orange soda to make
1/2 glass in tall glass.

Add 1 scoop ice cream and wait for soda fizzing to subside.
Pour in splash of seltzer to cut sweetness. Add second scoop
ice cream and drizzle in enough orange soda to fill glass.
Garnish with whipped cream and orange slice.

■ Orange Crush Soda is a great refresher when arriving home
   after a Big Orange win.

Marjorie Bradley, Greeneville, Tennessee

BIG ORANGE APRICOT SALAD

Serves 18

1 (20-ounce) can crushed pineapple
2 (3-ounce) packages apricot gelatin
2 cups buttermilk
1 cup chopped pecans
12 ounces whipped topping

Bring crushed pineapple to a boil in saucepan. Remove from
heat and add gelatin; mix to dissolve. Cool.

Stir in buttermilk and pecans. Fold in whipped topping. Pour
into 9x13-inch dish. Chill, covered in plastic wrap, until gelatin
is firm.

■ This salad from Ruth D. Brown is my most requested recipe.
   It keeps well in the refrigerator for 4 to 5 days.

Martha Chase Holt, Knoxville, Tennessee

BIG ORANGE SALAD

Serves 12

> 2 (11-ounce) cans mandarin oranges, drained
> 2 (15-ounce) cans crushed pineapple
> 1 (16-ounce) can sliced peaches, drained
> 1 cup sour cream
> 12 ounces whipped topping
> 5 tablespoons orange drink mix
> 1/2 cup chopped pecans (optional)

Mix mandarin oranges, pineapple and peaches in bowl.

Blend sour cream, whipped topping and drink mix in bowl. Fold in fruit and pecans.

Cover and refrigerate for 12 hours before serving. Serve in lettuce-lined plates.

Barbara M. Handley, Maryville, Tennessee

BIG ORANGE GELATIN SALAD

Serves 18

> 1 (20-ounce) can crushed pineapple
> 1/4 cup sugar
> 1 (6-ounce) package orange gelatin
> 2 cups cold water
> 2 cups shredded sharp Cheddar cheese
> 1 cup pecans (optional)
> 12 ounces whipped topping

Mix undrained crushed pineapple with sugar in saucepan. Bring to a boil. Remove from heat. Add gelatin, stirring to dissolve.

Add cold water and pour into serving dish. Chill until partially set. Stir in cheese and pecans; fold in whipped topping. Chill until set.

Beth Siphers Wendell, East Stone Gap, Virginia

Football has been part of Beth's heritage, as her father attended UT games "as far back as I can remember." Beth graduated from UT in 1949 with a business degree and received her master's degree there in 1956. She and her family attended the last two UT bowl games and have season tickets for all UT home games.

117

MANDARIN ORANGE SALAD

Serves 4

1 (11-ounce) can mandarin oranges
1/4 teaspoon salt
1 (6-inch) cinnamon stick
1/2 teaspoon whole cloves
1 (6-ounce) package orange gelatin
2 cups water
3 tablespoons lemon juice
1/2 cup pecans

Drain mandarin oranges, reserving juice. Combine reserved juice with enough water to measure 1 3/4 cups in saucepan. Add salt and spices.

Simmer, covered, for 10 minutes. Let mixture stand, covered, for 10 minutes. Strain into bowl. Mix in gelatin until dissolved. Add 2 cups water and lemon juice. Chill until partially set. Fold in oranges and pecans. Chill until ready to serve.

Evelyn Whitehead, Elizabethton, Tennessee

BIG ORANGE CHICKEN SALAD

Serves 6

3 (5-ounce) cans boned white meat chicken, drained
1 1/2 cups thinly sliced celery
1 (11-ounce) can mandarin oranges, drained
1 cup chopped walnuts
3/4 cup mayonnaise
1 teaspoon salt

Combine chicken, celery, oranges and walnuts. Add mayonnaise and salt; toss lightly. Chill until serving time. Serve with crackers on a bed of lettuce or on croissants.

Becki Hammond, Knoxville, Tennessee

ORANGE AND WHITE CHICKEN

Serves 8

8 boneless skinless chicken breasts
1/4 cup butter or margarine
1 cup finely chopped onion
2 cloves of garlic, minced
1 (8-ounce) jar orange marmalade
2 tablespoons steak sauce
1 cup shredded Gruyère or other white cheese

Rinse chicken and pat dry. Saute in butter in heavy skillet over medium heat until chicken is lightly browned on each side. Remove chicken to ovenproof 9x13-inch casserole dish.

Sauté onion and garlic in pan drippings until onion starts to brown. Add marmalade and steak sauce; stir just until mixed. Pour mixture over chicken. Sprinkle cheese evenly on top.

Bake at 400 degrees for 15 to 20 minutes or until chicken is fully cooked. Serve hot.

Walter and Anne Lambert, Knoxville, Tennessee

Becki Hammond and her husband, Gibbs, are thirty-year UT football fans. Gibbs is chaplain for the Knoxville Fire Department; watching UT football games is his favorite pastime. Becki prepares Big Orange Chicken Salad on game days.

119

ORANGE NUGGETS

Serves 8

2 pounds carrots, scraped, sliced
1 large onion, diced
1 (10-ounce) can tomato soup
1 cup sugar
1/2 cup vegetable oil
3/4 cup white vinegar
1/2 teaspoon dry mustard
2 tablespoons Worcestershire sauce
1/2 teaspoon salt
1/4 teaspoon pepper

Cook carrots in water to cover in saucepan until tender; drain. Combine onion with carrots in large bowl.

Combine tomato soup, sugar, oil, vinegar, dry mustard, Worcestershire sauce, salt and pepper in bowl. Pour over carrots and onion; mix well.

Chill, tightly covered, for 8 hours. Serve cold.

Anne Dalton (1968), Knoxville, Tennessee

APRICOT ORANGE BREAD

Serves 12

1 (6-ounce) package dried apricots
2 cups sifted flour
1 teaspoon salt
1/2 teaspoon baking soda
2 tablespoons butter
1 cup sugar
1 egg
1/2 cup orange juice
1/4 cup milk
1/2 cup pecans

Grease loaf pan and sprinkle with sugar. Wash apricots and cover with warm water in bowl. Let stand for 20 minutes. Drain and cut into small pieces.

Sift flour, salt and baking soda into medium bowl. Cream butter and sugar in mixer bowl until light. Add egg and beat until fluffy. Stir in orange juice and milk.

Stir in sifted dry ingredients. Add apricots and pecans; mix well.

Pour into prepared loaf pan. Bake at 350 degrees for 1 hour. Remove to wire rack to cool. Store, wrapped in foil, for 8 hours before serving.

Annie Classon (1988), Chattanooga, Tennessee

ORANGE BLOSSOM MUFFINS

Serves 12

   1 egg, slightly beaten
   1/4 cup sugar
   1/2 cup orange juice
   2 tablespoons salad oil or melted shortening
   2 cups baking mix
   1/2 cup orange marmalade
   1/2 cup chopped pecans
   Spicy Topping

Combine egg, sugar, orange juice and salad oil in medium bowl. Add baking mix; beat for 30 seconds. Stir in marmalade and pecans. Fill greased or paper-lined muffin cups 2/3 full.

Sprinkle with Spicy Topping. Bake at 400 degrees for 20 to 25 minutes or until golden brown.

Spicy Topping

   1/4 cup sugar
   1 1/2 tablespoons flour
   1/2 teaspoon cinnamon
   1/4 teaspoon nutmeg
   1 tablespoon butter or margarine

Combine sugar, flour, cinnamon and nutmeg in bowl; cut in butter until crumbly.

Mrs. John B. Harris, Goodlettsville, Tennessee

ORANGE YOGURT COFFEE CAKE

Serves 8

1 (2-layer) package yellow cake mix
8 ounces orange yogurt
1 egg, beaten
1/2 cup golden raisins
3 tablespoons sugar
1/2 teaspoon cinnamon

Mix cake mix, yogurt, egg and raisins in large bowl. Spoon into greased 8x8-inch pan. Mix sugar and cinnamon and sprinkle on top of batter.

Bake at 350 degrees for 30 minutes. Serve warm.

Marcella Thomas Epperson, Johnson City, Tennessee

PUMPKIN MUFFINS

Serves 4

1 cup pumpkin
3/4 cup vegetable oil
1 cup sugar
2 eggs, beaten
1/2 cup raisins
1/4 cup walnuts
1 1/2 cups sifted flour
1 teaspoon each baking powder and baking soda
1 teaspoon cinnamon
Salt to taste

Mix pumpkin, oil, sugar and eggs in medium bowl.

Rinse raisins and walnuts in hot water; drain. Mix flour, dry ingredients, raisins and walnuts in bowl. Fold in pumpkin mixture; mix well. Pour into greased muffin cups.

Bake at 350 degrees for 20 minutes or slightly longer for less moist muffins.

Frances D. Clabough, Maryville, Tennessee

123

PUMPKIN BREAD

Serves 16

1 1/2 cups sugar
1/2 cup vegetable oil
2 eggs
1/2 (16-ounce) can pumpkin, mashed
1 3/4 cups flour
3/4 teaspoon baking powder
1 teaspoon baking soda
1/3 teaspoon salt
2/3 teaspoon cloves
2/3 teaspoon nutmeg
2/3 teaspoon allspice
3/4 teaspoon cinnamon
1/2 teaspoon vanilla extract
1/3 cup water

Combine sugar, oil and eggs in large bowl; mix well.

Stir pumpkin into sugar mixture. Combine in bowl with flour, baking powder, baking soda, salt, cloves, nutmeg, allspice and cinnamon; mix well. Add vanilla and water; stir.

Pour into 2 greased and floured 5x9-inch pans.

Bake at 350 degrees for 1 hour.

■ This recipe has long been a favorite of the UT community. There were several requests to include it in this cookbook.

Department of Dining Services, UT Knoxville

MANDARIN ORANGE DESSERT

Serves 8

1 (10-ounce) package vanilla wafers
1 (14-ounce) can sweetened condensed milk
Juice of 2 lemons
1 (11-ounce) can mandarin oranges, drained
8 ounces whipped topping

Line bottom and side of 8x8-inch baking dish with vanilla wafers. Combine condensed milk and lemon juice in bowl; stir until thickened. Add mandarin oranges. Spread over vanilla wafers in prepared dish.

Layer additional vanilla wafers over orange mixture; spread with whipped topping. Garnish with wafer crumbs. Chill for 2 hours before serving.

You may substitute crushed pineapple for mandarin oranges.

Sue Lay, Oneida, Tennessee

ORANGE SHERBET

Serves 16

1 (20-ounce) can crushed pineapple
1 (6-ounce) package nonfat dry milk
1 (12-ounce) can sweetened condensed milk
6 (12-ounce) cans carbonated orange drink

Mix pineapple, dry milk, condensed milk and 1 can orange drink in large bowl. Pour into ice cream freezer; add orange drink to fill line. Freeze until firm.

Mary Helton, Knoxville, Tennessee

BIG ORANGE CAKE

Serves 12

1 1/2 cups sugar
1/2 cup shortening
2 eggs
2 cups sifted cake flour
1/4 teaspoon salt
1 tablespoon baking cocoa
3/4 cup buttermilk
1 1/2 ounces red food coloring
1/2 ounce yellow food coloring
1 teaspoon each vanilla extract and vinegar
1 teaspoon baking soda
Creamy Frosting

Cream sugar and shortening in medium mixer bowl. Beat in eggs. Fold in flour and salt gradually. Add next 7 ingredients; mix well.

Spoon into 3 greased and floured 8-inch cake pans. Bake at 350 degrees for 35 minutes. Cool on wire rack. Spread Creamy Frosting between layers and over top and side of cake. Store in refrigerator.

Creamy Frosting

1 cup milk
1/4 cup flour
1/2 teaspoon salt
1 cup sugar
1/2 cup butter and shortening
1 teaspoon vanilla extract

Combine 1/4 cup of the milk with flour and salt in saucepan; mix well. Add remaining milk. Cook until mixture thickens, stirring constantly. Chill for 2 hours.

Cream sugar, butter and shortening in medium mixer bowl until fluffy. Mix in vanilla and chilled mixture. Chill for 2 hours.

Mary Ann Harding, Germantown, Tennessee

MANDARIN ORANGE CAKE

Serves 12

1 (2-layer) package yellow cake mix
1/2 cup margarine
4 eggs
1 (11-ounce) can mandarin oranges
Creamy Pineapple Frosting

Combine cake mix, margarine, eggs and undrained mandarin oranges in medium mixer bowl; mix well. Beat at medium speed for 3 minutes.

Pour into 2 greased 9-inch cake pans. Bake at 350 degrees for 35 minutes or until layers test done. Split layers horizontally and spread Creamy Pineapple Frosting between layers and over top and side of cake. Chill until serving time.

Creamy Pineapple Frosting

1 (4-ounce) package instant vanilla pudding mix
8 ounces whipped topping
1 (20-ounce) can crushed pineapple

Combine pudding mix, whipped topping and undrained pineapple in bowl; mix well.

Jeanne Eldridge, Crossville, Tennessee

Laverne and Ethel Pearl Wheeler of Crab Orchard are true Big Orange fans; of the thirty-seven members of the Wheeler clan (children, grandchildren, great-grandchildren and their spouses), all are Tennessee fans and nine have graduated from UT. On fall Saturdays, family members gather around the television to cheer the home team. Those who make the journey to Knoxville to watch home games usually stop by the Wheeler home place after games, where Mandarin Orange Cake is a favorite.

127

ORANGE CAKE

Serves 12

Juice of 1 orange
1 cup packed brown sugar
1/2 cup margarine, softened
1 cup sugar
2 eggs
1 teaspoon baking soda
2/3 cup buttermilk
2 cups sifted flour
Grated orange rind
1/2 pound raisins
8 ounces whipped topping

Combine orange juice and brown sugar in small bowl; set aside.

Cream margarine and sugar in large mixing bowl. Add eggs 1 at a time, mixing well. Dissolve baking soda in buttermilk; add to egg mixture. Fold in flour. Stir in grated orange rind and raisins.

Spoon into ungreased baking dish. Bake at 350 degrees for 35 minutes.

Remove from oven. Pour orange juice and brown sugar mixture over cake. Serve hot with whipped topping.

Evelyn Whitehead, Elizabethton, Tennessee

ORANGE SLICE CAKE

Serves 14

8 ounces dates
1 pound candy orange slices
2 cups pecans
31/2 cups flour
1 cup margarine, softened
2 cups sugar
4 eggs
1/2 cup buttermilk
1 teaspoon baking soda
1 cup flaked coconut
Orange Glaze

Cut dates, orange slices and pecans into small pieces. Toss with a small portion of the flour in bowl. Set aside.

Cream margarine and sugar in medium mixer bowl; beat in eggs 1 at a time. Add buttermilk; mix well. Sift remaining flour with baking soda; add to creamed mixture. Fold in chopped pecans, dates and orange slices; mix well. Stir in coconut.

Pour into greased and floured bundt pan. Bake at 300 degrees for 11/2 hours or until cake tests done. Pour Orange Glaze over hot cake. Cool in pan. Invert onto cake plate.

Orange Glaze

2 cups confectioners' sugar
1 cup orange juice
2 teaspoons grated orange rind

Combine confectioners' sugar, orange juice and orange rind in bowl; mix well.

Marjorie Bradley, Greeneville, Tennessee
Marilyn Davenport, Sevierville, Tennessee
Pat Norris Harrison, Greeneville, Tennessee
Lance, Lucille, Randy and Kathy Pless, Greeneville, Tennessee

TANGY ORANGE CAKE

Serves 12

> 2 eggs
> 2 cups sugar
> 2 cups flour
> 2 teaspoons baking soda
> 1/2 teaspoon salt
> 2 (11-ounce) cans mandarin oranges, drained
> Brown Sugar Topping

Combine eggs, sugar and flour in large bowl; mix well. Stir in baking soda, salt and mandarin oranges. Pour into greased and floured bundt pan.

Bake at 350 degrees for 35 minutes. Cool slightly. Invert onto cake plate. Pierce cake with fork. Pour Brown Sugar Topping over cake. Garnish with whipped topping.

Brown Sugar Topping

> 3/4 cup packed brown sugar
> 3 tablespoons milk
> 2 tablespoons butter

Combine brown sugar, milk and butter in saucepan; mix well. Bring to a boil, stirring constantly.

Lee Miller, Knoxville, Tennessee

TENNESSEE ORANGE CAKE

Serves 12

- 1/3 cup butter, softened
- 1/3 cup shortening
- 1 1/2 cups sugar
- 3 eggs
- 2 1/4 cups sifted flour
- 2 1/2 teaspoons baking powder
- 1 teaspoon salt
- 1/2 cup milk
- 1/2 cup orange juice
- 1 cup flaked coconut
- 1 1/2 teaspoons grated orange rind
- Orange Filling

Cream butter, shortening and sugar in medium mixer bowl until fluffy. Beat in eggs. Sift flour, baking powder and salt together. Add to creamed mixture alternately with milk and orange juice, ending with flour and mixing well after each addition. Stir in flaked coconut and orange rind. Pour into 2 greased 9-inch cake pans.

Bake at 350 degrees for 30 minutes. Remove to wire rack to cool. Spread Orange Filling between layers.

Orange Filling

- 1 cup sugar
- 1/4 cup cornstarch
- 1/2 teaspoon salt
- 2 tablespoons butter
- 1 cup orange juice
- 2 tablespoons grated orange rind
- 1 1/2 tablespoons lemon juice

Mix sugar, cornstarch, salt, butter, orange juice, orange rind and lemon juice in saucepan. Bring to rolling boil. Boil for 1 minute, stirring constantly. Cool.

Michelle Foster, Lebanon, Tennessee

131

BIG ORANGE POUND CAKE

Serves 12

    1 cup butter, softened
    1/2 cup shortening
    3 cups sugar
    7 eggs
    2 teaspoons vanilla extract
    1 ounce orange food coloring
    3 cups flour
    1/4 teaspoon salt
    1 cup evaporated milk
    Cream Cheese Frosting

Cream butter, shortening and sugar in large mixer bowl until light. Beat in eggs 1 at a time. Add vanilla and food coloring. Add mixture of flour and salt alternately with evaporated milk to creamed mixture, mixing well after each addition.

Pour batter into greased and floured 10-inch bundt pan. Bake at 325 degrees for 1 hour and 20 minutes or until a wooden pick inserted in center comes out clean. Cool in pan for 15 minutes; invert onto cake plate and allow to cool completely. Frost with Cream Cheese Frosting. Garnish with candy orange slices or other candies.

Cream Cheese Frosting

    1/2 cup butter, softened
    6 ounces cream cheese, softened
    1 teaspoon vanilla extract
    1 (1-pound) package confectioners' sugar, sifted
    2 tablespoons (about) milk

Combine butter and cream cheese in medium bowl; mix until smooth. Stir in vanilla. Add confectioners' sugar; beat until creamy, adding enough milk to make of desired consistency.

April L. Burt, Greeneville, Tennessee

ORANGE-GLAZED POUND CAKE

Serves 12

1 cup shortening
2 cups sugar
4 eggs
1 teaspoon baking soda
1 1/2 cups buttermilk
4 cups flour
1 cup chopped dates
1 cup chopped candy orange slices
1 cup chopped pecans
Orange Glaze

Cream shortening and sugar in large mixer bowl. Add eggs, beating constantly.

Dissolve baking soda in buttermilk, Add to creamed mixture alternately with flour, mixing well after each addition. Add dates, candy orange slices and pecans; mix well. Pour into greased and floured bundt pan.

Bake at 300 degrees for 1 1/2 hours. Pierce top of cake with fork. Pour Orange Glaze gradually over top of hot cake. Let cake stand for 8 hours before removing from pan.

Orange Glaze

1 1/2 cups sugar
1 cup orange juice

Mix sugar and orange juice in saucepan. Bring to a boil and cook for 3 to 4 minutes or until of desired consistency.

Mae Burke, Fall Branch, Tennessee

133

CREAMY ORANGE POUND CAKE

Serves 16

1 1/2 cups margarine, softened
8 ounces cream cheese, softened
3 cups sugar
6 eggs
3 cups flour
1/4 teaspoon salt
1 tablespoon orange extract

Cream margarine and cream cheese in medium bowl until smooth. Add sugar and beat until light and fluffy. Add eggs, stirring constantly. Stir in flour, salt and orange extract.

Pour into greased and floured bundt pan. Place cake in cold oven. Bake at 300 degrees for 2 hours.

Barbara Duncan Nave (1974), Montgomery, Alabama

Barbara and her family have lived in Alabama for twenty-six years, but remain loyal UT fans. This recipe was adapted from one they found in Alabama, thus requiring a name and flavoring change.

ORANGE SPONGE CAKE

Serves 12

2 eggs, beaten
1 cup sugar
1 tablespoon grated orange rind
1/4 cup orange juice
1/4 cup water
11/4 cups sifted cake flour
11/4 teaspoons baking powder
1/4 teaspoon salt

Beat eggs in bowl until thick. Add sugar gradually, beating constantly. Add orange rind, juice and water. Sift flour, baking powder and salt together; fold gradually into egg mixture.

Pour into ungreased 8x8x2-inch cake pan. Bake at 350 degrees for 40 minutes.

■ This recipe was one of Doug's mother's. It can also be used for cupcakes.

Doug and JoAnne Dickey, Knoxville, Tennessee

Doug Dickey became head coach at UT in December, 1963. He coached the Vols from 1964 to 1969 and compiled a 46-15-4 record, before being named head coach at Florida. Doug was head coach at Florida from 1970 to 1978, and was assistant head coach at Colorado in 1979. He became athletic director for UT in 1985, and put top priority on bringing UT's athletic facilities to a level that "would rival any in the nation."

SWEET ORANGE NUGGETS

Serves 50

1 (2-layer) package orange cake mix
3 eggs
1/3 cup vegetable oil
1 cup orange juice
1 (11-ounce) can mandarin oranges, drained, chopped
Orange Glaze

Combine cake mix, eggs, oil and orange juice in large mixer bowl; mix well. Fold in oranges.

Pour into paper-lined small muffin cups.

Bake at 350 degrees for 10 to 15 minutes or until muffins test done. Cool on wire rack; remove from pans. Dip muffins into Orange Glaze.

Orange Glaze

2 cups confectioners' sugar
1 cup orange juice

Mix confectioners' sugar and orange juice in saucepan. Bring to boil, stirring constantly.

Joyce Willoughby, Gallatin, Tennessee

ORANGE WAFER BALLS

Makes 36

2 1/2 cups crushed vanilla wafers
1 cup (about) confectioners' sugar
1 cup finely chopped pecans
2 tablespoons baking cocoa
1/4 cup orange juice
2 tablespoons grated orange rind
3 tablespoons light corn syrup
1 cup confectioners' sugar

Joy Postell is the coach of the Vol cheerleaders.

Combine crushed vanilla wafers, 1 cup confectioners' sugar, chopped pecans, baking cocoa, orange juice, orange rind and corn syrup in medium bowl; mix well.

Shape into 1-inch balls on surface sprinkled with 1 cup confectioners' sugar, coating well.

■ Store in airtight container. These will keep for up to one month. You may omit the baking cocoa for "really" orange balls.

Marilyn Davenport, Sevierville, Tennessee
Robbie J. Melton, Livingston, Tennessee
Joy M. Postell, Knoxville, Tennessee

137

BIG ORANGE BARS

Makes 35

1 1/2 cups flour
1 teaspoon baking powder
Salt to taste
1 1/2 cups quick-cooking oats
1 cup packed brown sugar
3/4 cup butter or margarine, sliced
3/4 cup apricot preserves

Combine flour, baking powder, salt, oats and brown sugar in medium bowl; mix well. Cut in butter until crumbly. Press 2/3 of the mixture into ungreased 7x11-inch pan.

Spread preserves evenly over top. Sprinkle remaining crumb mixture over preserves; press lightly.

Bake at 350 degrees for 35 minutes. Cool. Cut into bars or squares.

Walter and Anne Lambert, Knoxville, Tennessee

Walter is the Associate Vice-President of Federal Affairs. He and Anne are both gourmet cooks. Walter writes a food column for the Knoxville newspaper and hosts a television cooking show.

BIG ORANGE COOKIE BARS

Makes 12

1/3 cup margarine, softened
1 cup packed dark brown sugar
1 egg
2 teaspoons vanilla extract
11/2 cups flour
1 tablespoon baking powder
1/2 teaspoon salt
1 teaspoon cinnamon
1/4 cup evaporated milk
3/4 cup finely chopped candy orange slices
1/2 cup miniature chocolate chips
1/4 cup chopped pecans
1/4 cup raisins

Cream margarine and brown sugar in medium mixer bowl until light. Add egg and vanilla; beat until fluffy. Combine flour, baking powder, salt and cinnamon in bowl. Add to creamed mixture alternately with evaporated milk, mixing well after each addition. Fold in orange candy, chocolate chips, pecans and raisins.

Spread batter evenly in greased and floured 8x8-inch baking pan. Bake at 350 degrees for 35 minutes. Cool in pan. Garnish with confectioners' sugar. Cut into small bars and store in tightly covered container.

Barbara Coleman (1959, 1966), Nashville, Tennessee

BIG ORANGE AMBER COOKIES

Serves 12

> 1 pound finely chopped candy orange slices
> 2 (3 1/2-ounce) cans flaked coconut
> 1 teaspoon each orange extract and vanilla extract
> 2 (14-ounce) cans sweetened condensed milk
> 1 cup pecans, finely chopped
> 3/4 cup (about) confectioners' sugar, sifted

Combine orange candy, coconut, flavorings, condensed milk and pecans in large bowl; mix well.

Spread in lightly greased 10x15-inch baking pan. Bake at 275 degrees for 30 minutes. Spoon hot mixture into confectioners' sugar in bowl.

Roll into 1-inch balls. Let stand until cool.

> *Walter and Anne Lambert, Knoxville, Tennessee*
> *Annie Martin Mitchell, Sparta, Tennessee*
> *Susan M. Perrin, Dayton, Tennessee*
> *Sarah and George Alvin Terry, Goodlettsville, Tennessee*

ORANGE CRINKLES

Makes 36

> 1 (2-layer) package orange cake mix
> 1/2 cup vegetable oil
> 2 eggs
> 1 tablespoon grated orange rind

Combine cake mix, oil, eggs and grated orange rind in medium bowl; mix well. Drop by spoonfuls onto ungreased baking sheet.

Bake at 350 degrees for 10 minutes or until light brown.

Cool on baking sheet for 1 minute; remove to wire rack to cool completely. You may top each slice with a pecan half before baking.

> *Marjorie Bradley, Greeneville, Tennessee*

ORANGE SLICE COCONUT COOKIES

Makes 48

11/2 cups packed brown sugar
1/2 cup shortening
2 eggs
1/2 teaspoon salt
1 teaspoon baking soda
2 cups flour
1/2 cup finely shredded coconut
1 pound candy orange slices, finely chopped
1 cup quick-cooking oats

Cream brown sugar and shortening in medium mixer bowl until light. Add eggs; mix well. Sift in salt, baking soda and 11/2 cups of the flour. Add coconut. Toss the orange candy with 1/2 cup flour in bowl. Add candy and oats to batter; mix well. Chill for 8 hours. Roll into balls. Place on cookie sheet; press with fork to flatten.

Bake at 350 degrees for 8 to 10 minutes or until golden brown.

■ We celebrate UT victories with Orange Slice Coconut Cookies, our adult children's favorite childhood dessert.

Connie Steele, Knoxville, Tennessee
Head, Department of Child and Family Studies
College of Human Ecology

BIG ORANGE CHESS PIE

Serves 6

1/2 cup butter or margarine, softened
1 cup sugar
3 eggs, beaten
3 tablespoons cornmeal
1 1/3 tablespoons grated orange rind
1/2 cup orange juice
1 tablespoon lemon juice
1 unbaked (9-inch) pie shell

Cream butter in medium mixer bowl. Add sugar gradually, beating constantly. Beat in eggs. Stir in cornmeal, orange rind, orange juice and lemon juice.

Spoon into pie shell. Bake at 350 degrees for 45 minutes or until knife inserted into center comes out clean.

Garnish with orange slice and mint sprig.

Kim Newman (1989), Maryville, Tennessee

MANDARIN ORANGE PIE

Serves 10

1 (14-ounce) can sweetened condensed milk
16 ounces whipped topping
1/4 cup lemon juice
1 cup chopped pecans
2 (11-ounce) cans mandarin oranges, drained
1 large or 2 small graham cracker pie shells

Combine condensed milk, whipped topping, lemon juice, pecans and oranges in large bowl; mix well.

Spoon into pie shell. Chill until serving time.

Anna Faye Ray, Ten Mile, Tennessee

TANGY BIG ORANGE PIE

Serves 8

1 (14-ounce) can sweetened condensed milk
1/2 cup orange breakfast drink mix
1 cup sour cream
1 cup whipped topping
1 (8-ounce) can mandarin oranges, drained
1 graham cracker pie shell

Combine condensed milk, drink mix, sour cream and whipped topping in medium bowl. Reserve several orange slices. Combine remaining orange slices with condensed milk mixture; mix well.

Spoon into pie shell. Top with reserved orange slices. Chill for 4 hours.

Susan Seaman, Piney Flats, Tennessee

BIG ORANGE SUMMER PIE

Serves 8

1 (3-ounce) package orange gelatin
3/4 cup boiling water
1/2 cup cold water
1 (8-ounce) can mandarin oranges, drained
8 ounces whipped topping
1 baked (9-inch) pie shell

Dissolve gelatin in boiling water in saucepan. Add cold water.

Cut mandarin orange slices into halves; add to gelatin. Stir in whipped topping.

Spoon into cooled pie shell. Chill for 2 hours or longer.

Mildred Serra, Knoxville, Tennessee

Susan and her husband became engaged at the 1990 UT Cotton Bowl game. UT played Susan's home team, the Arkansas Razorbacks. At that time, they believed the two teams would only meet once in a lifetime—only to have Arkansas join the SEC a few months later! The recipe for Tangy Big Orange Pie was developed during their first football season as a married couple, and it has been a big hit.

ORANGE SURPRISE TARTS

Serves 10

1 (5-ounce) milk chocolate bar
2 tablespoons milk
10 pastry tart shells, baked
3 egg yolks, slightly beaten
1/4 cup orange juice
1 teaspoon lemon juice
1/2 cup sugar
1/8 teaspoon salt
2 cups whipped topping
1 tablespoon grated orange rind

Melt chocolate bar with milk in double boiler over hot water; stir until smooth. Cool slightly and spread in tart shells. Place egg yolks in double boiler; add orange and lemon juices gradually. Stir in sugar and salt. Cook until thickened, stirring constantly. Cool to room temperature.

Fold in whipped topping and orange rind. Spoon into large bowl. Chill, covered, until serving time.

Spoon into tart shells just before serving. Garnish with fresh orange slices.

Mary J. Rice, Troy, Tennessee

AN ORANGE SUNSET

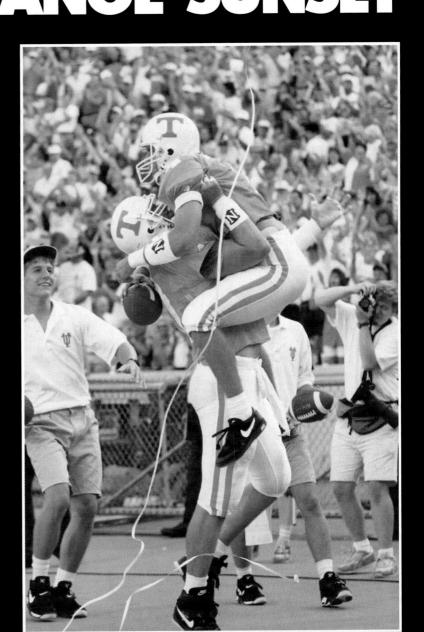

When Doug Dickey was at Tennessee as coach, the Tennessee- Alabama game again became the biggest of the year in this part of the nation. He says that, "When Sports Illustrated came in on Tuesday to cover a game to be played on Saturday, I knew we had something special working in this series. I can tell you it was great being a part of the competition that existed then and exists now between the two programs. To win made it memorable for a lifetime.

"I can't think of a more important win for me or the Tennessee program while I was there than the win over Alabama in 1967. That was it for me. It was a turning point in our program. Without a doubt, it made a statement that we were doing OK, after a bad lull.

"The 1967 football team was not a collection of outstanding football players. We had some good ones, of course. You have to have good ones to win. But our strength lay in being a TEAM. The players had unity. They had purpose. They thought of themselves as a team."

CHEESE STRAWS

Makes 36

> 1 cup fresh bread crumbs
> 2/3 cup flour
> 1 cup shredded Cheddar cheese
> 1 tablespoon melted butter
> 1/2 teaspoon salt
> Cayenne pepper to taste
> 1/8 teaspoon white pepper
> 2 tablespoons (about) milk

Combine bread crumbs, flour, cheese, butter, salt, cayenne pepper and white pepper in bowl; mix well. Add enough milk to make of desired consistency.

Roll or pat 1/4 inch thick on floured surface. Cut into 1/4x4-inch strips. Place on baking sheet. Bake at 375 degrees until golden brown.

Edith E. Abernathy, Augusta, Georgia

UN-OFFENSIVE CHEESE BALL

Serves 24

> 16 ounces cream cheese, softened
> 2 cups shredded sharp Cheddar cheese, at room
> temperature
> 1 (6-ounce) can crushed pineapple, drained
> 2 teaspoons seasoned salt
> 1 teaspoon curry powder

Beat cream cheese, Cheddar cheese, pineapple, seasoned salt and curry powder in mixer bowl until mixed. Shape into a ball.

Chill, covered, for 2 to 3 days prior to serving to enhance flavor.

Let stand at room temperature for 1 1/2 hours before serving. Garnish with maraschino cherry on top; roll in chopped fresh parsley. Serve with assorted party crackers.

Janet S. Proffitt, Maryville, Tennessee

Edith Abernathy and her husband were at UT from 1946 to 1949. Her recipe for Cheese Straws is from *Volunteer Recipes*, a collection of recipes from prominent women of the United States, collected by the Home Economics Club of UT in 1948. This recipe is from Jessie W. Harris, dean of the College of Home Economics. Edith still has a copy of the book, which "was used many times while we lived in a trailer on the side of The Hill in Hillside Village."

In 1992, Dana Reed (1973) encouraged the students in her comprehension development class at West View Middle School in Morristown to enter a contest sponsored by the Paul Newman Food Company and *Good Housekeeping* magazine. They used Newman's Own Sockarooni Spaghetti Sauce to create Bagelroonies. As one of the seven national winners, they received a trip for four to New York, $1,000 spending money, and $10,000 to donate to their favorite charity, which was the Area 10 Special Olympics. In succeeding years, they won additional awards, totaling $22,500 for the Morristown area from Mr. Newman.

BAGELROONIES

Serves 6

6 onion bagels, cut into halves
6 tablespoons soft-spread margarine
1 (14-ounce) jar Newman's Own Sockarooni Spaghetti Sauce
1 (8-ounce) package Canadian bacon slices, chopped
1 (16-ounce) package shredded mozzarella cheese

Spread cut sides of bagel halves with margarine. Spread about 3 tablespoons Sockarooni Sauce over each; sprinkle with bacon and mozzarella cheese. Arrange bagel halves on baking sheet. Broil until bubbly.

For variety, sprinkle sliced mushrooms, green olives, black olives or jalapeños over mozzarella cheese. Sprinkle freshly grated Parmesan cheese over mozzarella cheese if desired.

Dana Reed's CDC-Special Education Class
Morristown, Tennessee

ROCKY TOP BREAD

Serves 16

1 (6-ounce) package Mexican corn bread mix
1/3 cup (about) milk
1 egg
1 Vidalia onion, coarsely chopped
1/4 each teaspoon paprika and red pepper
1 teaspoon Worcestershire sauce
Vegetable oil for frying

Combine corn bread mix, milk, egg, onion, paprika, hot red pepper and Worcestershire sauce in bowl; mix well.

Drop by tablespoonfuls into hot oil in skillet. Fry until brown on both sides, flattening with spatula while frying; drain.

■ Serve with lime wedges and Big Orange Bourbon drinks.

Gene H. Scott, Lewisburg, Tennessee

CLARKSVILLE EGGNOG

Serves 5

6 egg yolks
1/2 cup sugar
2 cups bourbon
2 tablespoons light rum
2 cups milk
2 cups half-and-half
6 egg whites
1/4 cup sugar
1 teaspoon grated nutmeg

Philip Tate's favorite memory is of The University of Tennessee thrashing of Miami in the 1986 Sugar Bowl.

Beat egg yolks and 1/2 cup sugar in mixer bowl until well mixed. Add bourbon and rum gradually, beating constantly until blended. Beat in milk and half-and-half.

Beat egg whites with 1/4 cup sugar in mixer bowl until stiff peaks form. Fold into egg yolks mixture, beating at low speed. Sprinkle with nutmeg.

Chill, covered, for 2 to 12 hours to enhance flavor. Pour into punch bowl; stir. Ladle into punch cups.

■ Every Christmas Eve, after my father got home from his mail route, he would "assist" my mother in making eggnog for the neighborhood party. He "assisted" by adding extra bourbon when my mother wasn't looking. My father was always at his best on Christmas Eve.

CMSgt. Philip R. Tate, Mascoutah, Illinois

OLD COLLEGE INN BLACK BEAN GUMBO

Serves 20

3^1/$_2$ pounds dried black beans
^{1}/$_2$ cup butter
^{1}/$_4$ cup flour
1 (10-ounce) can Cheddar cheese soup
4 ounces Cheddar cheese, shredded
2 teaspoons cumin
1 teaspoon garlic powder
Salt and pepper to taste

Sort and rinse black beans. Combine with enough water to cover in stockpot. Soak for 24 hours; drain. Add water to cover. Cook for 1 to 1^1/$_2$ hours or until black beans are tender.

Heat butter in saucepan until melted. Stir in flour gradually. Cook until of roux consistency, stirring constantly.

Add soup, cheese, cumin and garlic powder to black beans; mix well. Stir in roux.

Cook until of desired consistency, stirring frequently. Season with salt and pepper.

John Staudifer, Knoxville, Tennessee

BEEF BURGER SOUP

Serves 6

- 1 pound ground chuck or ground round
- 1/4 cup minced onion
- 2 cloves of garlic, minced
- 3 cups canned tomato juice
- 1 (6-ounce) can vegetable juice cocktail
- 2 (10-ounce) cans cream of celery soup
- 1 cup water
- 2 cups shredded carrots
- 1/4 teaspoon salt
- 1 bay leaf
- 1/4 teaspoon marjoram
- Pepper to taste

In his senior season at UT in 1985, Daryl appeared relegated to a backup role behind Tony Robinson. When Robinson went out with a knee injury in the Alabama game, Daryl led the Vols to six victories and a tie, including a 35–7 win over Miami in the Sugar Bowl, where he was named MVP!

Brown ground chuck with onion and garlic in stockpot, stirring until ground chuck is crumbly; drain.

Combine tomato juice, vegetable juice cocktail, soup and water in bowl; mix well. Stir into ground chuck mixture. Add carrots, salt, bay leaf, marjoram and pepper; mix well.

Simmer for 1 hour or until carrots are tender and soup is of desired consistency, stirring occasionally. Discard bay leaf. Ladle into soup bowls.

■ JoAnne, the wife of Doug and mother of Daryl, says that her children were reared on this soup, which is actually orange in color.

JoAnne and Daryl Dickey
Knoxville, Tennessee

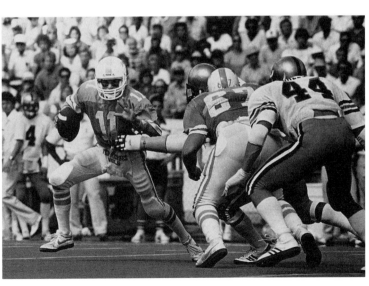

151

COMPANY CHILI

Serves 6

12 ounces ground round steak
4 ounces hot sausage
1/2 small onion, chopped
1 (46-ounce) can tomato juice
1 (16-ounce) can light red kidney beans
3 tablespoons chili powder

Brown ground round and sausage with onion in skillet, stirring until ground round and sausage are crumbly; drain.

Bring tomato juice, kidney beans and chili powder to a boil in stockpot. Add ground round mixture; mix well.

Simmer, covered, for 1 to 3 hours or until of desired consistency, stirring frequently. Ladle into chili bowls. Serve leftovers in taco salad and nachos.

John (1960), Marsha and Julia Swift, Hermitage, Tennessee

HODGEPODGE

Serves 12

1 1/2 pounds ground chuck
3/4 cup chopped onion
1 cup chopped celery
1 clove of garlic, minced
3 (10-ounce) cans minestrone soup
3 cups water
1 (31-ounce) can pork and beans
1 tablespoon Worcestershire sauce
1 teaspoon oregano
Salt and pepper to taste

Brown ground chuck with onion, celery and garlic in stockpot, stirring until meat is crumbly; drain. Stir in remaining ingredients. Simmer for 20 minutes or until of desired consistency, stirring occasionally. Ladle into soup bowls.

Becky Hartman, Knoxville, Tennessee

OLD SOUTH BRUNSWICK STEW

Serves 12

1 (2 1/2- to 3-pound) beef roast
1 (2 1/2- to 3-pound) pork roast
Salt to taste
1 (16-ounce) can cream-style white corn
1 (28-ounce) can chopped tomatoes
Worcestershire sauce to taste

Combine roasts and salt with enough water to cover in stockpot. Simmer for 2 1/2 hours or until roasts are very tender. Remove roasts to platter to cool, reserving broth.

Cut or shred beef and pork into bite-size pieces. Add beef and pork, corn and tomatoes to reserved broth; mix well. Bring to a boil; reduce heat.

Simmer for 30 to 40 minutes or until of desired consistency, stirring occasionally. Season with Worcestershire sauce and salt.

■ Add a green salad and hot crusty bread and serve before or after UT football games or take to a tailgate party. You may freeze in meal-size portions for future use.

Barbara Pelot, Knoxville, Tennessee

Billy Henry is senior administrative assistant and director of spring sports in the UT Athletic Department. He has been a coach and administrator in college athletics since 1960. Martha is a graduate of the College of Human Ecology and has been an instructor there. She is currently Food Service Director for Maryville Schools.

SHERRIED BEEF

Serves 8

3 pounds beef stew meat
2 (10-ounce) cans cream of mushroom soup
3/4 cup sherry
1/2 envelope onion soup mix

Arrange stew meat in baking dish. Pour mixture of soup, sherry and soup mix over meat.

Bake, covered, at 325 degrees for 3 hours. Serve over hot cooked rice or noodles.

Billy and Martha Anne Henry, Knoxville, Tennessee

153

MEAT LOAF

Serves 8

1 small onion, chopped
1/4 cup chopped green bell pepper
1 stalk celery, chopped
1 tablespoon olive oil
1 1/2 pounds ground chuck
1 carrot, grated
1 egg, beaten
1/4 teaspoon basil
1/4 teaspoon rosemary
2 slices dry bread, crumbled
1 (8-ounce) can tomato sauce
2 slices bacon, cut into 2-inch pieces

Sauté onion, green pepper and celery in olive oil in skillet for 2 minutes; drain.

Combine onion mixture, ground chuck, carrot, egg, basil, rosemary, bread crumbs and 3/4 of the tomato sauce in a bowl; mix well. Shape into a round loaf. Place in 2 1/2-quart baking dish sprayed with nonstick cooking spray. Top with bacon; drizzle with remaining tomato sauce.

Bake at 350 degrees for 1 1/2 hours. Add chopped plum tomatoes when in season for variety.

Mary Jane Hays, Knoxville, Tennessee

MEXICAN DINNER

Serves 10

2 pounds ground beef
1 large onion,
   chopped
2 cloves of garlic,
   minced
2 (8-ounce) cans
   tomato sauce
5 1/2 tomato sauce
   cans water
3 (6-ounce) cans
   tomato paste
1/4 cup sugar
2 to 4 tablespoons
   chili powder
2 teaspoons
   oregano
2 teaspoons cumin
2 teaspoons salt
2 teaspoons MSG
1 tablespoon
   chopped fresh
   basil
1 tablespoon chopped fresh sage
1 tablespoon chopped fresh mint

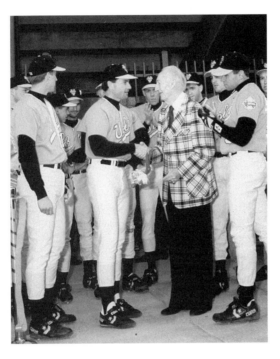

Lindsey Nelson (1941) is synonymous with baseball and sports broadcasting in general. He covered major league baseball for 25 years with NBC, the New York Mets and the San Francisco Giants. The Volunteer baseball stadium is named in his honor.

Brown ground beef in skillet, stirring until crumbly; drain.

Bring onion, garlic, tomato sauce, water, tomato paste, sugar, chili powder, oregano, cumin, salt and MSG to a boil in stockpot, stirring occasionally. Stir in ground beef; reduce heat.

Simmer for 1 hour or until of desired consistency, stirring occasionally. Stir in basil, sage and mint. Spoon over corn chips or serve in taco shells. Serve with chopped onion, chopped green pepper, sliced stuffed green olives, shredded lettuce and shredded cheese.

Lindsey Nelson, Knoxville, Tennessee

155

LASAGNA

Serves 8

1 (12-ounce) package
  lasagna noodles
3 pounds lean
  ground beef
1 large onion,
  chopped
1 (16-ounce) can
  chopped tomatoes
1 (12-ounce) can
  tomato paste
1 (10-ounce) can
  tomato soup
2 teaspoons salt
1 teaspoon oregano
3 tablespoons flour
Garlic salt to taste
6 ounces grated
  Romano cheese
12 ounces mozzarella cheese, sliced

Tim Irwin played offensive tackle at Tennessee from 1978 to 1980 and played with the Minnesota Vikings and Tampa Bay Buccaneers in the NFL. He is a graduate of Central High School and has been a strong supporter of the Knoxville Boy's and Girl's Clubs. He says, "I will never forget beating Notre Dame in Knoxville in 1979."

Prepare lasagna noodles using package directions. Rinse with cold water; drain.

Brown ground beef with onion in skillet, stirring until ground beef is crumbly; drain. Stir in tomatoes, tomato paste, soup, salt, oregano, flour and garlic salt.

Simmer for 15 minutes, stirring occasionally.

Layer ground beef mixture, Romano cheese, mozzarella cheese and noodles 1/2 at a time in baking dish. Bake, covered, at 350 degrees for 1 hour.

Tim Irwin, Knoxville, Tennessee

SPAGHETTI MEAT SAUCE

Serves 40

- 3 pounds ground beef
- 1 pound hot sausage
- 2 medium onions, chopped
- 2 large green bell peppers, chopped
- 1 (29-ounce) can tomato sauce
- 1 (12-ounce) can tomato paste
- 2 (48-ounce) cans spaghetti sauce
- I (6-ounce) can sliced mushrooms
- 2 cups water
- 2 envelopes spaghetti sauce mix
- 1 teaspoon salt
- 1/2 teaspoon black pepper
- 3/4 teaspoon chopped garlic
- 1/2 teaspoon garlic powder
- 3/4 teaspoon chili powder
- 1/8 teaspoon ground red pepper
- 1/4 teaspoon paprika

Brown ground beef and sausage with onions in skillet, stirring until ground beef and sausage are crumbly. Pour into colander; rinse with hot water and drain.

Combine green peppers, tomato sauce, tomato paste, spaghetti sauce, mushrooms, water, spaghetti sauce mix, salt, black pepper, garlic, garlic powder, chili powder, red pepper and paprika in 8-quart saucepan; mix well. Stir in ground beef mixture. Bring to a boil; reduce heat.

Simmer for 1 hour or until of desired consistency, stirring frequently. Spoon over hot cooked spaghetti.

Nancy S. Starnes, Knoxville, Tennessee

ORANGE PORK CHOPS WITH RICE

Serves 6

1¹/3 cups instant rice
1 cup orange juice
6 thick (4-ounce) pork chops
Salt and pepper to taste
1 (10-ounce) can chicken soup

Place rice in shallow baking dish. Pour orange juice over rice.

Brown pork chops in skillet; drain. Season with salt and pepper. Arrange pork chops over rice. Pour soup over prepared layers.

Bake, covered, at 350 degrees for 45 minutes; remove cover. Bake for 10 minutes longer.

You may substitute chicken broth for soup.

Lance, Lucille, Randy and Kathy Pliss, Greeneville, Tennessee

BAKED CHICKEN AND TAMALES

Serves 8

1 tablespoon butter
2 (16-ounce) cans tamales
6 chicken breast halves, cooked, chopped
3 (8-ounce) cans tomato sauce
1 cup sour cream
2 cups shredded Cheddar cheese

Spread butter over bottom and sides of 8x10-inch baking dish. Layer tamales and chicken in prepared dish.

Pour mixture of tomato sauce, sour cream and cheese over prepared layers.

Bake at 350 degrees for 20 to 30 minutes or until bubbly.

Rena Jones Johnson (1959), Sparta, Tennessee

SPICED ROAST CHICKEN

Serves 4

1 (3¹/₂-pound) chicken
1 onion, finely chopped
2 tablespoons olive oil
1 teaspoon garam masala or curry powder
4 ounces button, brown or chestnut mushrooms, chopped
1 cup each coarsely grated parsnips and grated carrots
1/4 cup minced walnuts
2 teaspoons chopped fresh thyme
1 cup fresh white bread crumbs
1 egg, beaten
Salt and pepper to taste
1/4 cup water
1 tablespoon margarine
2/3 cup marsala

Rinse chicken and pat dry.

Sauté onion in olive oil in saucepan for 2 minutes or until tender. Stir in garam masala. Cook for 1 minute, stirring constantly. Stir in mushrooms, parsnips and carrots. Cook for 5 minutes, stirring constantly. Remove from heat. Stir in walnuts, thyme, bread crumbs, egg, salt and pepper. Stuff mixture into chicken; truss.

Place chicken breast side down in roasting pan; pour water around chicken. Roast at 375 degrees for 45 minutes; turn chicken. Dot with margarine. Roast for 45 minutes or until meat thermometer inserted in thickest part of thigh registers 185 degrees. Transfer to warm platter.

Discard fat from roasting pan. Add marsala, stirring to deglaze pan. Boil for 1 minute or until liquid is slightly reduced, stirring constantly. Adjust seasonings.

Remove skin from chicken; carve. Garnish with thyme and watercress sprigs. Serve with stuffing, flavored pan juices and seasonal vegetables.

Tipper Gore, Washington, D.C.

159

CHICKEN CASSEROLE

Serves 8

64 butter crackers
1/4 cup margarine
4 to 6 chicken breast halves, cooked, chopped
1 (8-ounce) can sliced water chestnuts, drained
Salt and pepper to taste
1 (10-ounce) can cream of mushroom soup
1 (10-ounce) can cream of chicken soup
1 cup sour cream
64 butter crackers, crumbled
1/4 cup margarine

Crumble 64 crackers in bottom of 9x13-inch baking dish; dot with 1/4 cup margarine. Arrange chicken over margarine; top with water chestnuts. Season with salt and pepper.

Spread mixture of soups and sour cream over prepared layers. Sprinkle with crumbled crackers; dot with 1/4 cup margarine.

Bake, loosely covered with foil, at 400 degrees for 30 minutes.

Nancy Galbreath and Marie Tinnon, Goodlettsville, Tennessee

Since 1940, the Tinnon family has been wearing the Orange and White. "As graduates and sidewalk alumni, we have marched with the General, Barnhill, Britton, Robinson, Wyatt, McDonald, Dickey, Battle, Majors and Fulmer. We have traveled with the Vols from Baton Rouge to California and all cities in between, and we even enjoyed the day we missed the exit to the Rose Bowl and ended up in Malibu. We say the three greatest things are God, Family and the Big Orange."

HOT CHICKEN SALAD

Serves 8

2 to 3 cups chopped cooked chicken
1 medium onion, finely chopped
2 cups chopped celery
1 (5-ounce) can sliced water chestnuts, drained
1 (4-ounce) can sliced mushrooms, drained
1 (2-ounce) jar diced pimento
1 (2-ounce) can sliced black olives
1/2 cup mayonnaise
1/2 (10-ounce) can cream of mushroom soup
Salt and pepper to taste
4 hard-cooked eggs, sliced
1 (10-ounce) can cream of chicken soup
3/4 cup crushed potato chips

Combine chicken, onion, celery, water chestnuts, mushrooms, pimento and olives in bowl; mix well. Stir in mayonnaise, mushroom soup, salt and pepper. Spoon into 9x13-inch baking dish.

Arrange egg slices over top. Spoon chicken soup evenly over layers; sprinkle with potato chips.

Bake at 350 degrees for 45 minutes.

You may add 4 ounces noodles cooked in chicken broth and the remaining 1/2 can cream of mushroom soup and serve 10 to 12 guests.

Peggy Hankins, Decherd, Tennessee

"Most memories will probably be submitted as 'Best Memories', but I have chosen to submit our worst one—one never forgotten. My husband, John, and I made plans to attend the UT-Penn State football game in Knoxville in 1971. However, these plans were interrupted on the Friday before the game by emergency surgery for John. Needless to say, he was miserable, not only because of the surgery but more so because of his inability to be present at the game. John slept through the game and missed one of Bobby Majors' greatest games. He will never forget missing UT's 31 to 11 victory over Penn State. But the victory did relieve some of his misery!"

MARYLAND CRAB CAKES

Serves 6

1 pound lump crab meat
1 cup soft bread crumbs
1 egg, lightly beaten
1/4 cup mayonnaise
1 tablespoon prepared mustard
1 teaspoon Worcestershire sauce
2 tablespoons minced fresh parsley
1/4 teaspoon white pepper
Tabasco sauce to taste
Vegetable oil for frying

Combine crab meat and bread crumbs in bowl; mix gently.

Combine egg, mayonnaise, mustard, Worcestershire sauce, parsley, white pepper and Tabasco sauce in bowl; mix well. Stir gently into crab meat mixture. Shape into 6 patties.

Chill, wrapped in plastic wrap, for 30 minutes.

Heat 1/4-inch oil in skillet to 350 degrees. Fry crab cakes in hot oil for 3 minutes per side or until golden brown; drain.

Serve with lemon wedges and tartar sauce with dill and capers.

Chef Don DeVore, The Painted Table, Knoxville, Tennessee

CRAWFISH CASSEROLE

Serves 4

1 (10-ounce) can tomatoes with green chiles
1 each onion and green bell pepper, chopped
1 pound crawfish tails
1/2 cup margarine
1 (7-ounce) package chicken Rice-A-Roni, cooked
1 (10-ounce) can cream of mushroom soup
1 cup shredded longhorn cheese

Process tomatoes in blender until coarsely chopped.

Sauté onion, green pepper and crawfish tails in margarine in skillet. Stir in rice, soup and tomatoes. Spoon into baking dish; sprinkle with cheese.

Bake at 350 degrees for 20 minutes. You may prepare in advance and bake just before serving or freeze for future use.

Joan Cronan, Knoxville, Tennessee

Joan Cronan is the Women's Athletic Director at UT. She is one of the fourteen members serving on the Executive Committee of the NCAA. She and her husband Tom were reared in "Cajun" country.

LOBSTER SAUCE FOR PASTA

Serves 6

16 ounces chunk lobster
1/2 small purple onion, chopped
Lemon pepper to taste
2 tablespoons olive oil
Florets of 1 bunch broccoli
1 red bell pepper, chopped
1 (6-ounce) can mushrooms, drained
3 tablespoons butter
2 tablespoons ranch salad dressing mix

Stir-fry lobster, onion and lemon pepper in olive oil in skillet. Remove to platter. Stir-fry broccoli, red pepper and mushrooms in skillet. Add lobster mixture; mix well. Stir in butter and salad dressing mix. Stir-fry over low heat until heated through. Serve over pasta.

Missy Kane, Knoxville, Tennessee

Missy Kane is currently a sports and fitness anchor for a Knoxville television station. She is a former member of the Lady Vol track team and a former Lady Vol assistant coach. She captained the cross-country and track and field team from 1973 to 1977.

163

CASSEROLE SAINT JACQUES

Serves 4

1 pound sea scallops, cut into halves
1 (3-ounce) can broiled mushrooms
1 cup dry white wine
1 small onion, thinly sliced
1 tablespoon minced fresh parsley
1 teaspoon salt
2 tablespoons butter
2 tablespoons lemon juice
2 tablespoons butter
1/4 cup flour
1 cup light cream
1/3 cup shredded Gruyère cheese
Pepper to taste
8 ounces cooked shrimp
8 ounces fresh crab meat
1 cup bread crumbs
1 tablespoon melted butter

UT

Linda Franz Cook, in only her third season at the helm of the Lady Vol golf team, in 1994 carried the team to NCAA championship contention. At the University of Missouri, she was a three-time USGA Women's National Qualifier.

Drain scallops and mushrooms, reserving liquid. Combine reserved liquid with enough water to measure 2 cups.

Bring white wine, onion, parsley and salt to a boil in saucepan. Stir in scallops; reduce heat. Simmer for 4 minutes, stirring occasionally. Add mushrooms, 2 tablespoons butter and lemon juice. Simmer until butter melts, stirring frequently.

Melt 2 tablespoons butter in saucepan. Stir in flour until blended. Add reserved liquid and cream; mix well. Cook over low heat until thickened, stirring constantly. Stir in cheese and pepper. Cook until cheese melts, stirring constantly. Add scallop mixture, mushrooms, shrimp and crab meat; mix gently. Heat just until bubbly, stirring frequently.

Spoon into 2-quart baking dish; sprinkle with mixture of bread crumbs and 1 tablespoon melted butter. Broil until brown.

Linda Franz Cook, Knoxville, Tennessee

FIERY CAJUN SHRIMP

Serves 4

    1 cup melted butter
    1/4 cup Worcestershire sauce
    1/4 cup ground pepper
    1 teaspoon rosemary
    1/4 teaspoon hot pepper sauce
    2 teaspoons salt
    1 clove of garlic, minced
    Juice of 1 lemon
    1 1/2 pounds unpeeled shrimp
    1 lemon, sliced

Mix butter, Worcestershire sauce, pepper, rosemary, hot pepper sauce, salt, garlic and lemon juice in bowl. Pour 1/4 cup of the sauce into large baking dish. Arrange shrimp and lemon slices over top. Drizzle with remaining sauce.

Bake at 400 degrees for 20 minutes or until shrimp turn pink, stirring 1 or 2 times.

Bob Bell, Springfield, Tennessee

PENNE JULIA

Serves 2

    3/4 cup Alfredo sauce
    1 cup grated Romano cheese
    1 ounce prosciutto, chopped
    2 tablespoons each peas and sliced mushrooms
    Salt and pepper to taste
    1 (8-ounce) package penne, cooked, drained

Bring the Alfredo sauce to a boil in a sauté pan over medium heat. Stir in cheese. Add prosciutto, peas, mushrooms, salt and pepper; mix well. Reduce heat. Cook until of desired consistency, stirring constantly. Spoon over hot cooked penne in bowl, tossing to coat.

Italian Market and Grill, Knoxville, Tennessee

During one period of Bob Bell's career, the television station where he worked engaged him for a play-by-play broadcast of a rival UT basketball game. He reports, "I was riding on this team's bus when we rolled onto the Tennessee campus for a game one late January night. It was a gorgeous Rocky Top night, every light on campus was on, and a soft sparkling snow was falling. Not keeping in mind whose bus I was on, I turned to the player sitting beside me and said, 'Isn't this a great place!' The young man gave me a stunned look and said, 'Yeah, I guess so...'"

165

BROCCOLI AND WALNUT PRIMAVERA

Serves 6

2 cups fresh spinach
2 teaspoons basil
2 cloves of garlic
1/4 cup grated Parmesan cheese
1/4 cup chopped walnuts
1/4 cup red wine vinegar
1 teaspoon salt
1/4 teaspoon pepper
2/3 cup olive oil
1 (12-ounce) package fettuccini
1 tablespoon olive oil
1 pint cherry tomatoes, cut into halves
1 bunch broccoli, cut into 1-inch pieces, blanched
1/2 cup sliced black olives
1/2 cup chopped walnuts

Process spinach, basil, garlic, cheese, 1/4 cup walnuts, wine vinegar, salt and pepper in food processor or blender until chopped. Add 2/3 cup olive oil in fine stream, processing constantly at high speed until thick and creamy.

Prepare fettuccini using package directions until al dente; drain. Toss with 1 tablespoon olive oil in bowl. Add tomatoes, broccoli, olives and 1/2 cup walnuts, tossing to mix.

Add 1/2 of the dressing to the pasta mixture, tossing to coat. Serve the remaining dressing with the pasta. Serve with grilled chicken or shrimp. Use leftover dressing on hot cooked pasta, salads or grilled meats.

Jennifer Webb, Knoxville, Tennessee

SPINACH MARIA

Serves 15

    5 (10-ounce) packages frozen chopped spinach
    4 1/2 cups milk
    1 1/2 pounds Velveeta cheese, chopped
    1 teaspoon dry mustard
    1 teaspoon granulated garlic
    1 1/2 teaspoons crushed red pepper
    1/2 medium yellow onion, finely chopped
    1 tablespoon butter
    6 tablespoons flour
    5 tablespoons melted butter
    1 cup shredded Monterey Jack cheese

Thaw spinach in refrigerator for 24 hours. Squeeze excess moisture from spinach.

Heat milk, Velveeta cheese, dry mustard, garlic and red pepper in double boiler over hot water, stirring frequently.

Sauté onion in 1 tablespoon butter in skillet for 3 minutes. Stir into cheese mixture. Cook until cheese is melted, stirring constantly; reduce heat.

Combine flour and 5 tablespoons melted butter in saucepan; mix well. Cook over low heat for 3 to 4 minutes or until of roux consistency, stirring constantly. Stir into cheese mixture. Cook until thickened, stirring constantly. Remove from heat. Let stand for 15 minutes. Stir in spinach. Spoon into large baking dish; sprinkle with Monterey Jack cheese.

Bake at 350 degrees for 12 to 15 minutes or until bubbly.

Paul Rentschler, Copper Cellar Restaurant, Knoxville, Tennessee

SPINACH-STUFFED TOMATOES

Serves 8

8 tomatoes
Salt to taste
2 (10-ounce) packages frozen chopped spinach
3/4 cup soft bread crumbs
8 slices crisp-fried bacon, crumbled
Nutmeg to taste
Garlic powder to taste
Pepper to taste
1 tablespoon butter
1/4 cup melted butter

Cut tops from tomatoes. Scoop out pulp to form shells, discarding pulp. Sprinkle inside cavity with salt. Invert to drain for 1 hour.

Cook spinach in saucepan just until thawed; drain. Combine spinach, bread crumbs, bacon, nutmeg, garlic powder, salt and pepper in bowl; mix well. Spoon into tomato shells. Arrange in baking dish coated with 1 tablespoon butter. Drizzle tomatoes with 1/4 cup melted butter.

Bake at 350 degrees for 20 minutes. Garnish each tomato with sour cream and sprig of dillweed.

Marian T. Hunter, Knoxville, Tennessee

U T

Marian's husband George played end on the Volunteer football team from 1936 to 1938. A native of Somerset, Kentucky, he had a successful career in the meat packing business and in banking before his retirement. He also served as the first president of the East Tennessee Chapter of the National Football Foundation and Hall of Fame.

GRITS FRITTERS

Serves 12

1 cup flour
1 teaspoon salt
1 teaspoon baking powder
1 egg, beaten
1 teaspoon chives
3/4 cup milk
1/4 cup shredded Cheddar cheese
1 cup cold cooked grits
1 (4-ounce) slice ham, finely chopped
2 dashes of Zack's Virgin Habanero Sauce
Vegetable oil for frying
1/2 cup white wine
Chopped parsley to taste
1 tablespoon chopped shallot
3/4 cup butter
2 to 3 tablespoons sour cream

Combine flour, salt, baking powder, egg, chives and milk in bowl; mix well. Stir in cheese, grits, ham and Zack's sauce. Chill, covered, for 8 to 12 hours.

Heat 1/4 inch vegetable oil in skillet over medium heat. Drop grits mixture by spoonfuls into hot oil. Fry for 2 to 4 minutes per side or until brown; drain.

Combine wine, parsley and shallot in saucepan. Cook over low heat until reduced by 1/2, stirring occasionally. Stir in butter until melted. Add sour cream; mix well. Serve over fritters.

You may shape the grits mixture into balls and roll in seasoned bread crumbs before frying.

John Hurt, Zack's Foods, Nashville, Tennessee

169

RIZ BISCUITS

Serves 12

> 1 envelope dry yeast
> 1 cup buttermilk, at room temperature
> 2 1/4 cups flour
> 1/2 teaspoon baking soda
> 1 tablespoon sugar
> 3 tablespoons shortening
> 1/4 cup melted butter

Dissolve yeast in buttermilk; mix well.

Sift flour, baking soda and sugar into bowl; mix well. Cut in shortening until crumbly. Stir in buttermilk mixture. Knead until smooth.

Roll dough 1/2 inch thick on lightly floured surface; cut with biscuit cutter. Brush tops with butter.

Arrange biscuits in stacks of 2 on baking sheet. Let rise for 1 1/2 hours.

Bake at 450 degrees for 12 minutes.

Faye Julian, Knoxville, Tennessee
Professor and Head, Speech Communication

HEARTY CHEESY BEEF CORN BREAD

Serves 6

> 1 tablespoon yellow cornmeal
> 8 ounces ground beef
> 1 cup yellow cornmeal
> 3/4 teaspoon salt
> 1/2 teaspoon baking soda
> 1 cup milk
> 1 (17-ounce) can cream-style corn
> 2 eggs, beaten
> 1/4 cup vegetable oil
> 2 cups shredded hoop cheese
> 1 large onion, finely chopped
> 2 to 4 jalapeños, seeded, chopped

Sprinkle 1 tablespoon cornmeal in bottom of greased 10-inch cast-iron skillet. Cook over medium heat until cornmeal is light brown. Set aside.

Brown ground beef in another skillet, stirring until crumbly; drain.

Combine 1 cup cornmeal, salt and baking soda in bowl; mix well. Stir in milk, corn, eggs and oil. Pour 1/2 of the batter into prepared skillet; sprinkle with cheese, onion, jalapeños and ground beef. Top with remaining batter.

Bake at 350 degrees for 50 to 55 minutes or until brown.

Bonnie W. Fritch, Dunlap, Tennessee

Bonnie is a graduate of the College of Human Ecology and an Extension Home Economist.

CORN LIGHT BREAD

Serves 12

 1 tablespoon bacon drippings
 2 cups cornmeal
 1 cup flour
 1 cup sugar
 1 teaspoon salt
 1 teaspoon baking soda
 2 cups buttermilk

Heat bacon drippings in loaf pan in 325-degree oven until hot.

Sift cornmeal, flour, sugar, salt and baking soda into bowl; mix well. Stir in buttermilk and bacon drippings. Spoon into loaf pan. Spoon hot bacon grease over batter.

Bake at 300 to 325 degrees for 1 hour or until bread tests done.

Bettye Jo Luton, Dyer, Tennessee

DARING DATES

Serves as many as you make

 Pitted Dates
 Bourbon
 Pecan halves, toasted
 Sugar

Soak dates in bourbon for 12 hours; drain. Stuff each date with pecan half; roll in sugar.

Store in airtight container.

Anna-Lee G. Cockrill, Nashville, Tennessee

DIRT CAKE

Serves 15

3 (4-ounce) packages instant vanilla pudding mix
4 3/4 cups milk
16 ounces cream cheese, softened
2/3 cup confectioners' sugar
16 ounces whipped topping
3 (20-ounce) packages chocolate sandwich cookies, crushed

Combine pudding mix and milk in bowl, stirring until blended. Beat cream cheese and confectioners' sugar in mixer bowl until smooth. Stir in pudding mixture and whipped topping.

Layer cookie crumbs and pudding mixture alternately in new flowerpot, beginning and ending with cookies. Garnish with silk flowers and gummy worms.

Dan Brooks, Maryville, Tennessee

EARTHQUAKE CAKE

Serves 16

1 cup chopped pecans
1 cup flaked coconut
1 (2-layer) package German chocolate cake mix
8 ounces cream cheese, softened
1 (1-pound) package confectioners' sugar
1/2 cup melted butter or margarine

Sprinkle pecans and coconut over bottom of 9x13-inch baking pan. Prepare cake mix using package directions. Spread evenly over prepared layer.

Beat cream cheese, confectioners' sugar and butter in mixer bowl until smooth. Spread evenly over cake batter; swirl to marbleize.

Bake at 350 degrees for 45 minutes. Cool on wire rack.

Annie Martin Mitchell, Sparta, Tennessee

Dan Brooks has been defensive line coach at Tennessee since 1994. He is a graduate of Western Carolina and received his masters degree from Florida.

173

HERSHEY CAKE

Serves 15

1 cup sugar
1/2 cup butter or margarine, softened
4 eggs
1 1/4 cups self-rising flour
1 (16-ounce) can Hershey's chocolate syrup
1 teaspoon vanilla extract
1 (10-ounce) package miniature marshmallows
1 1/2 cups sugar
3 tablespoons (heaping) baking cocoa
1/2 cup (or more) milk
1/2 cup margarine
1 teaspoon vanilla extract
1 (1-pound) package confectioners' sugar

Cream 1 cup sugar and 1/2 cup butter in mixer bowl until light and fluffy. Add eggs 1 at a time, beating well after each addition. Stir in flour, chocolate syrup and 1 teaspoon vanilla. Spoon into 9x13-inch baking pan.

Bake at 350 degrees for 30 minutes. Sprinkle marshmallows over baked layer.

Combine 1 1/2 cups sugar, baking cocoa, milk and 1/2 cup margarine in saucepan; mix well. Cook for 3 minutes, stirring constantly. Remove from heat. Add 1 teaspoon vanilla and confectioners' sugar, beating until of spreading consistency. Spread evenly over marshmallows.

Joy Shires, Knoxville, Tennessee

SIX-FLAVOR POUND CAKE

Serves 20

3 cups sugar
1/2 cup shortening
1/2 cup butter, softened
5 eggs, beaten
3 cups cake flour, sifted
1 teaspoon baking powder
1/4 teaspoon salt
1 cup milk
1 teaspoon orange extract
1 teaspoon lemon extract
1 teaspoon rum extract
1 teaspoon vanilla extract
1 teaspoon coconut extract
1 teaspoon butter flavoring

Beat sugar, shortening and butter in mixer bowl until creamy. Add eggs; mix well. Mix cake flour, baking powder and salt. Add to creamed mixture alternately with milk, mixing well after each addition. Stir in flavorings. Spoon into greased and floured 10-inch tube pan.

Bake at 350 degrees for 1 hour. Glaze with your favorite icing if desired.

This cake freezes well for up to 2 months.

Emma J. Tapley, Murfreesboro, Tennessee

175

REGAS RED VELVET CAKE

Serves 12

2 1/2 cups cake flour
1 teaspoon baking soda
1/3 teaspoon salt
1/2 cup baking cocoa
1 cup plus 2 tablespoons butter, softened
2 cups sugar
4 eggs
1 cup buttermilk
1 teaspoon vanilla extract
5 teaspoons red food coloring
Red Velvet Frosting
1/4 cup red-tinted flaked coconut

Sift cake flour, baking soda, salt and baking cocoa together.

Cream butter and sugar in mixer bowl until light and fluffy. Add eggs 1 at a time, beating well after each addition. Add dry ingredients and buttermilk 1/2 at a time, beating well after each addition. Stir in vanilla and red food coloring. Spoon into three 9-inch greased and floured cake pans.

Bake at 350 degrees for 30 minutes or until layers test done. Invert onto wire rack to cool. Spread Red Velvet Frosting between layers and over top and side of cake. Sprinkle top with coconut.

Red Velvet Frosting

1 (1-pound) package confectioners' sugar
1 cup butter, softened
1/2 cup whipping cream
1 teaspoon vanilla extract

Beat confectioners' sugar, butter, whipping cream and vanilla in mixer bowl until fluffy, scraping sides occasionally.

Regas Restaurant, Knoxville, Tennessee

SNICKERDOODLES

Makes 72

1 cup shortening
1 1/2 cups sugar
2 eggs
2 3/4 cups flour
1/2 teaspoon salt
1 teaspoon baking soda
2 teaspoons cream of tartar
2 teaspoons cinnamon
1/4 cup sugar

Cream shortening and 1 1/2 cups sugar in mixer bowl until light and fluffy. Beat in eggs. Add sifted mixture of flour, salt, baking soda and cream of tartar; mix well. Chill, covered, until firm.

Shape dough into 1-inch balls; roll in mixture of cinnamon and 1/4 cup sugar. Place 2 inches apart on ungreased cookie sheet.

Bake at 400 degrees for 8 to 10 minutes or until light brown. Remove to wire rack to cool.

Mae Burke, Fall Branch, Tennessee

FUDGE PIES WITH CHOCOLATE SAUCE

Serves 12

1 (1-ounce) square unsweetened chocolate
1/2 cup butter
1 cup sugar
2 eggs
1/2 cup sifted flour
1 teaspoon vanilla extract
1/2 cup chopped pecans (optional)
1 pint vanilla ice cream
Chocolate Sauce

Melt chocolate in double boiler over hot water. Cream butter in mixer bowl until light. Add sugar gradually, beating until fluffy. Beat in eggs 1 at a time. Stir in chocolate.

Add flour and vanilla; mix well. Stir in pecans. Spoon into 2 greased 9-inch pie plates.

Bake at 325 degrees for 30 minutes. Cool in pans. Cut into wedges to serve. Serve with ice cream and Chocolate Sauce.

■ This pie always satisfies a hungry governor!

Chocolate Sauce

1/4 cup butter
2 (1-ounce) squares unsweetened chocolate
1 cup sugar
1 cup evaporated milk
1 teaspoon vanilla extract

Melt butter and chocolate in saucepan over low heat. Stir in sugar until dissolved. Add evaporated milk; mix well.

Bring to a boil and cook for 3 minutes or until smooth and slightly thickened, stirring constantly. Stir in vanilla. Cool to room temperature.

Martha Sundquist, Nashville, Tennessee

Martha is the wife of Don Sundquist, who won the 7th District congressional seat in Memphis in 1982; he was re-elected five times. In 1994, he was elected Governor of Tennessee.

A LIGHT SLICE

Pat Head Summitt remembers each of her teams as different and special in its own way. "The 1976-77 team took us to our first National Tournament (AIAW) and finished third. I remember this team as being our best defensive team, and they had huge hearts.

"The '87 Championship was especially exciting because of such a decisive win over Louisiana Tech. The score of 67 to 44 remains vivid in my mind today. This team will be remembered as a team of over-achievers.

"The '89 Championship team was mentally tough and managed to do—by most people's standards—what they were supposed to do: win the National Championship. No squad has been tougher under pressure.

"In '91, we were down by 5 points with 1:25 to go and the team refused to lose. I remember Dena Head hitting two free throws with seven seconds remaining in regulation play to put the game in overtime. We went on to capture our third National Championship.

"The '94-'95 team is the most exciting transition team to date, and the team that has successfully handled the toughest schedule in the history of the program."

LOW-FAT MEXICAN DIP

Serves 16

1 (16-ounce) can nonfat refried beans
1 (16-ounce) jar salsa
1 cup nonfat sour cream
1 cup shredded low-fat sharp Cheddar cheese
2 (16-ounce) packages baked tortilla chips

Combine refried beans and salsa in medium saucepan; mix well. Cook over low heat, stirring until smooth. Pour into 8x8-inch baking pan. Spread with sour cream; top with cheese.

Bake at 350 degrees for 20 minutes or until cheese melts. Garnish with lettuce and tomato. Serve warm with tortilla chips.

Lauren Howell, Oak Ridge, Tennessee

MEXICAN BEEF DIP

Serves 12

1 pound lean ground beef
1/2 cup chopped onion
1 (8-ounce) jar hot taco sauce
3/4 teaspoon oregano
1 clove of garlic, minced
1/4 cup tomato catsup
1 teaspoon sugar
1/3 cup grated Parmesan cheese
8 ounces cream cheese or Neufchâtel cheese, cubed

Brown ground beef with onion in skillet, stirring until ground beef is crumbly; drain. Add taco sauce, oregano, garlic, catsup, sugar and Parmesan cheese; mix well.

Stir in cream cheese cubes. Serve with tortilla chips or crackers or spoon into a wide-mouth thermos to take to tailgate parties. For an even lighter dip, substitute turkey for the ground beef.

Janet S. Proffitt, Maryville, Tennessee

BROCCOLI SOUP

Serves 4

- 1 1/2 pounds broccoli
- 3 tablespoons butter or margarine
- 1 medium onion, chopped
- 4 cups chicken stock or bouillon, heated
- 1/2 cup low-fat or skim milk
- 1 egg yolk
- 1/2 teaspoon salt
- 1/8 teaspoon pepper

Cut broccoli florets into sections; cut stems into slices. Combine butter and onion in 3-quart microwave-safe dish. Microwave on High for 5 minutes or until brown, stirring once. Stir in chicken stock and broccoli. Microwave, covered, on High for 15 minutes or until broccoli is tender.

Beat milk and egg yolk in small bowl. Add to broccoli mixture, gradually, mixing well. Microwave on High for 2 minutes. Let stand, covered, for 5 minutes. Add salt and pepper.

Purée in blender until smooth. Garnish with chopped parsley or green onions.

You may purée only a portion of the broccoli mixture for chunkier soup.

Bess C. Hammock, Knoxville, Tennessee

CHARLIE'S DIET CHILI

Serves 6

1 pound lean ground beef
1 medium onion, chopped
2 cups sliced celery
1/2 cup chopped green bell pepper
1/2 teaspoon garlic salt
1 (15-ounce) can kidney beans
2 (16-ounce) cans tomatoes
2 1/2 teaspoons salt
1 teaspoon chili powder
1 bay leaf

Charlie Daniels is a well known country and western musician. He has performed on several occasions with the UT band at half-time shows in Neyland Stadium.

Brown ground beef with onion in heavy saucepan, stirring until ground beef is crumbly; drain. Add celery, green pepper, garlic salt, undrained beans, undrained tomatoes, salt, chili powder and bay leaf.

Simmer, covered, over low heat for 2 hours. Remove bay leaf. Serve hot.

This soup freezes well.

Charlie Daniels, Lebanon, Tennessee

LOW-FAT CORN AND POTATO CHOWDER

Serves 12

8 to 10 red potatoes, cubed
2 to 3 green onions, chopped
1 (10-ounce) can whole kernel corn
1 (6-ounce) can mushrooms
Salt and pepper to taste

Cook potatoes and green onions in water to cover in large saucepan until tender. Reduce heat and add corn, mushrooms, salt and pepper. Simmer for 45 minutes over low heat.

You may leave the skin on the potatoes to add flavor and nutrients to soup. Thin with skim milk if necessary for desired consistency.

Dick and Susan Williams, Knoxville, Tennessee

Dick Williams was captain of the 1968 UT football team. He is now president of Plateau Group, Inc. in Crossville, Tennessee. Dick's favorite UT memory is of leading the Vols through the "T" every Saturday. "Nothing will ever top that!"

184

FRUIT SALAD

Serves 8

 1 medium avocado, sliced
 2 apples, sliced
 1 tablespoon lemon juice
 1/2 head Bibb lettuce
 1 (11-ounce) can mandarin oranges
 3/4 cup sugar
 1 tablespoon dry mustard
 1/3 medium onion, finely grated
 1 cup corn oil
 1 tablespoon each poppy seeds and salt
 1/3 cup red wine vinegar

Toss avocado and apple slices with lemon juice and a small amount of water in small bowl to prevent browning; drain. Arrange drained avocado and apple slices on lettuce leaves on salad plates. Top with oranges.

Combine remaining ingredients in blender container. Process until smooth. Drizzle over salad.

Barbara Coleman (1959, 1966), Nashville, Tennessee

UT FRUIT BOWL

Serves 10

 1 (20-ounce) can pineapple chunks
 2 cups honeydew melon cubes and watermelon cubes
 2 cups watermelon cubes
 2 medium oranges, sliced
 1 cup seedless green grapes
 1 cup sliced strawberries
 2 medium apples, sliced
 2 medium bananas, sliced

Combine all ingredients in large resealable container. Chill until serving time.

Kimberly Loveday, Chattanooga, Tennessee

185

NUTTY PINEAPPLE COLESLAW

Serves 8

2 1/2 cups shredded green cabbage
1 1/2 cups shredded red cabbage
3/4 cup chopped red bell pepper
1 (8-ounce) can crushed pineapple, drained
1 cup nonfat sour cream
2 tablespoons sugar
1 tablespoon dry mustard
3 tablespoons cider vinegar
1/8 teaspoon salt
2 tablespoons unsalted dry-roasted peanuts, chopped

Combine green and red cabbages and bell pepper in large bowl; toss well. Mix crushed pineapple, sour cream, sugar, mustard, vinegar and salt in small bowl. Fold into cabbage mixture.

Chill, covered, for 4 hours or longer. Sprinkle with peanuts just before serving.

Ella H. Nunley, Martin, Tennessee

TOMATO ASPIC

Serves 6

1 small package sugar-free lemon gelatin
1/2 cup boiling water
1 (16-ounce) can chunky tomatoes
1 cup cottage cheese

Dissolve gelatin in boiling water in saucepan. Add tomatoes, mixing well. Stir in cottage cheese. Pour into tube mold.

Chill for 8 hours or until firm. Invert onto serving plate.

Bess C. Hammock, Knoxville, Tennessee

PASTA SALAD

Serves 6

1 (8-ounce) package rotini or shell macaroni
Salt to taste
1 cup sliced mushrooms
1/4 cup chopped green pepper
1/4 cup sliced green onions
Vinaigrette Dressing
1 1/2 cups seedless red grapes, halved

Cook pasta in boiling salted water in saucepan using package directions; drain.

Toss pasta with mushrooms, green pepper, green onions and Vinaigrette Dressing in bowl.

Chill, covered, for 8 hours. Add grape halves and toss.

Vinaigrette Dressing

1/4 cup vegetable oil
3 tablespoons white wine vinegar
1 tablespoon minced parsley
1/2 teaspoon salt
1/4 teaspoon dried oregano
Pepper to taste
Tabasco sauce to taste

Combine oil, white wine vinegar, parsley, salt, oregano, pepper and Tabasco sauce in bowl; blend well.

Montez Medling, Greenfield, Tennessee

PASTA WITH BLACK BEANS AND ARTICHOKE HEARTS

Serves 6

> 1 tablespoon olive oil
> 1 cup sliced green onions
> 3/4 teaspoon dried whole oregano
> 1/4 teaspoon salt
> 1/8 teaspoon crushed red pepper
> 1/8 teaspoon black pepper
> 1 clove of garlic, minced
> 2 (14-ounce) cans no-salt-added tomatoes, undrained, chopped
> 1 (15-ounce) can black beans, drained
> 4 cups hot cooked macaroni or other small pasta
> 1 (14-ounce) can artichoke hearts, drained, quartered

Heat oil in large non-stick skillet over medium heat. Add green onions and sauté for 6 minutes. Stir in oregano, salt, red pepper, black pepper, garlic and tomatoes. Simmer, covered, for 10 minutes over low heat. Stir in beans. Simmer, covered, for 5 minutes longer.

Toss bean mixture, pasta and artichoke hearts in a large bowl. Serve warm or at room temperature.

You may also top with grated Parmesan or shredded mozzarella cheese.

Dorothy Doolittle, Knoxville, Tennessee

UT

Dorothy Doolittle became head coach for the women's track and field and cross country teams in 1987. She was one of the coaches for the 1992 Summer Olympic games.

LOW-FAT POCKET SANDWICHES

Serves 10

    4 cups cooked ham or turkey strips
    4 cups packed torn leaf lettuce
    2 medium tomatoes, chopped
    2 cups Cheddar cheese, cubed
    5 (6-inch) pocket bread rounds
    Pocket Sandwich Dressing

Combine ham, lettuce, tomatoes and cheese in large bowl; toss gently. Cut bread rounds into halves and spoon ham mixture into pockets. Drizzle Pocket Sandwich Dressing over filling.

You may add 2 1/2 cups alfalfa sprouts if desired.

Pocket Sandwich Dressing

    1/4 cup vegetable oil
    2 tablespoons olive oil
    2 tablespoons red wine vinegar
    2 teaspoons dried salad herbs
    1/2 teaspoon dry mustard
    1 clove of garlic, minced
    1/2 teaspoon salt
    1/4 teaspoon pepper

Combine vegetable oil, olive oil, vinegar, salad herbs, dry mustard, garlic, salt and pepper. Blend well. Store in airtight jar in refrigerator.

Wanda Brown, Hermitage, Tennessee
Bettye Erb, Old Hickory, Tennessee
Submitted by Don Richardson, Dean of AES

CRUNCHY CHICKEN SALAD

Serves 10

1/4 cup each vegetable oil and vinegar
1/4 cup sugar
1 teaspoon salt
1/2 teaspoon pepper
2 tablespoons poppy seeds
4 chicken breasts, cooked, cubed
3 green onions, chopped
1 (4-ounce) package sliced almonds
1 ((8-ounce) can chow mein noodles

Combine oil, vinegar, sugar, salt, pepper and poppy seeds in bowl; mix well. Pour into glass baking dish. Chill for 4 hours.

Combine chicken, green onions and almonds in bowl. Add dressing; mix gently. Chill, covered, for 4 hours. Add noodles at serving time; toss gently. Serve on bed of leaf lettuce or tomatoes. Garnish with orange slice.

Evelyn Stout, Old Hickory, Tennessee

Evelyn and her husband attend all UT home games and many UT games away from home with three other couples—"our 'extended family.' We are known by friends as the Tennessee Gang, and we look forward each season to special times at the games."

PAPRIKA CHICKEN

Serves 6

11/2 cups water
2 tablespoons each vinegar and margarine
1/2 teaspoon paprika
Salt and pepper to taste
6 boneless skinless chicken breasts

Combine water, vinegar, margarine, paprika, salt and pepper in saucepan; blend well. Bring to a boil; reduce heat and simmer for 8 minutes. Pour into glass baking dish.

Rinse chicken and pat dry. Arrange in prepared dish.

Bake, covered, at 325 degrees for 2 to 21/2 hours or until chicken is tender.

Gloria Ray, Knoxville, Tennessee

Gloria Ray served as the Lady Vols' first athletic director from 1977 to 1984. The Gloria Ray Leadership Award named in her honor is presented annually to a Lady Vol basketball player. She is now president and CEO for Knoxville Sports Corporation.

BIG ORANGE FISH WITH SHRIMP

Serves 4

  3 cups water
  1 pound unpeeled shrimp
  4 orange roughy fillets
  2 cloves of garlic, crushed
  1/4 cup lime juice
  1 medium onion, chopped
  1 medium green bell pepper, chopped
  3 tomatoes, peeled, chopped
  2 jalapeño peppers, seeded, chopped
  1 1/2 tablespoons olive oil
  1 bay leaf
  1/2 teaspoon dried oregano
  1/4 teaspoon ground cinnamon
  2 tablespoons capers

Bring water to a boil in saucepan over medium heat. Add shrimp. Cook for 5 minutes; drain and rinse with cold water. Chill for 4 hours. Peel and devein shrimp.

Place fish fillets in 2-quart casserole. Sprinkle with garlic and lime juice; set aside.

Saute onion, green pepper, tomatoes and jalapeño peppers in olive oil in medium skillet until vegetables are tender. Add bay leaf, oregano and cinnamon. Spoon over fish fillets. Sprinkle with capers.

Bake at 425 degrees for 20 minutes. Add shrimp and bake for 4 minutes longer. Remove bay leaf before serving.

Chris Blanton, Madison, Tennessee

WHOLE WHEAT VEGETABLE LASAGNA

Serves 8

2 tablespoons extra-virgin olive oil
1 tablespoon unsalted butter
1 tablespoon each chopped garlic and basil
1/4 cup chicken stock
1 cup low-fat or skim milk
1 1/2 tablespoons each arrowroot and cold water
Salt substitute and white pepper to taste
Florets of 1/2 head broccoli
2 tablespoons chopped onion
6 mushrooms, sliced
1 tablespoon butter
1 each zucchini and carrot, shredded
1/2 (8-ounce) package whole wheat lasagna noodles, cooked
4 ounces low-fat mozzarella cheese
1/4 cup grated Parmesan cheese

Combine olive oil, 1 tablespoon unsalted butter, garlic and basil in small saucepan. Cook over medium heat for 2 minutes; do not brown. Add chicken stock and milk; bring to a boil over high heat. Stir in mixture of arrowroot and cold water. Cook until thickened, stirring constantly. Add salt substitute and white pepper.

Blanch broccoli in boiling water in saucepan for 1 minute or until tender-crisp. Sauté onion and mushrooms in 1 tablespoon butter in skillet until tender. Add broccoli, zucchini and carrot. Sauté briefly. Remove from heat; drain.

Spread 1/3 of the basil sauce in small baking dish. Layer with half the lasagna noodles, vegetable mixture and half the mozzarella cheese. Add half the remaining basil sauce, remaining noodles, remaining basil sauce and remaining mozzarella cheese. Sprinkle with Parmesan cheese.

Bake at 350 degrees for 15 to 20 minutes or until cheese is brown. Let stand for 20 minutes before serving.

Hersel Widener, Johnson City, Tennessee

VOL VEGGIES

Serves 8

2 cups each broccoli florets and cauliflowerets
2 carrots, sliced 1/4 inch thick
2 zucchini, sliced 3/4 inch thick
5 cloves of garlic, cut into halves (optional)
2 tablespoons virgin olive oil
Salt and freshly ground pepper to taste
1 tablespoon grated Parmesan cheese

Combine broccoli, cauliflower, carrots, zucchini, garlic and olive oil in large bowl; toss to coat well. Spread in shallow baking pan.

Bake at 450 degrees for 20 minutes or until tender-crisp, stirring once or twice. Sprinkle with salt, pepper and cheese.

Edna Threlkeld Scales, Nashville, Tennessee

STUFFED ZUCCHINI

Serves 6

3 medium zucchini
3/4 cup sliced fresh mushrooms
1/4 cup chopped onion
3/4 cup chopped tomato
1 1/4 teaspoons dried Italian seasoning
1/8 teaspoon pepper
1 tablespoon grated Parmesan cheese

Steam zucchini, covered, for 12 minutes or until tender-crisp. Slice zucchini lengthwise, leaving stems intact. Remove pulp, reserving 1/4-inch shells. Dice pulp and set aside.

Sauté mushrooms and onion in skillet sprayed with nonstick vegetable spray. Stir in zucchini pulp, tomato, Italian seasoning and pepper. Cook over low heat, stirring constantly. Spoon into zucchini shells and sprinkle cheese over tops. Place on baking sheet.

Bake at 350 degrees for 25 minutes. Garnish with fresh thyme.

Ella H. Nunley, Martin, Tennessee

193

LOW-FAT CORN BREAD

Serves 12

> 1 cup self-rising cornmeal
> 8 ounces plain yogurt
> 1 (8-ounce) can cream-style corn
> 1 tablespoon liquid margarine
> 1/4 cup egg substitute

Combine cornmeal, yogurt, corn, margarine and egg substitute in bowl; mix well. Spoon into hot greased medium skillet.

Bake at 450 degrees for 20 to 25 minutes, or until corn bread tests done.

Susan Williams, Knoxville, Tennessee

Susan Williams (1967) was associate athletic director for development for the UT Lady Vols. Her favorite memories are of being part of two national basketball championships in 1989 and 1991.

LOW-FAT CAKE AND FRUIT

Serves 16

> 1 small package sugar-free pistachio pudding and pie filling mix
> 2 cups milk
> 16 ounces whipped topping
> 1 lemon angel food cake
> 1 cup sliced kiwifruit and strawberries

Prepare pudding mix with 2 cups milk using package directions. Allow to cool for 10 minutes. Add whipped topping; mix well.

Cut cake horizontally into 2 layers. Layer cake, pudding mixture and fruit 1/2 at a time on serving plate.

You may substitute other flavors of cake and pudding mix.

Sharon K. Tubbs, Humboldt, Tennessee

CHOCOLATE AND AMARETTO CHEESECAKE

Serves 12

6 chocolate wafers, finely crushed
1 1/2 cups light cream cheese
1 cup sugar
1 cup 1% cottage cheese
6 tablespoons baking cocoa
1/4 cup flour
1/4 cup amaretto
1 teaspoon vanilla extract
1/4 teaspoon salt
1 egg
2 tablespoons miniature semisweet chocolate chips
3 (1-ounce) squares semisweet chocolate

Sprinkle chocolate wafer crumbs in bottom of 7-inch springform pan; set aside. Combine cream cheese, sugar, cottage cheese, baking cocoa, flour, amaretto, vanilla and salt in food processor container; process until smooth. Add egg and process until just blended. Fold in chocolate chips. Pour into prepared pan.

Bake at 300 degrees for 65 to 70 minutes or until cheesecake is set. Cool in pan on wire rack. Chill, covered, for 8 hours.

Melt chocolate squares in double boiler over hot water. Pour melted chocolate onto waxed paper, spreading into 3-inch wide strip. Let stand until cool but not firm. Pull vegetable peeler across chocolate to make curls.

Place cheesecake on serving plate; remove side of pan. Top with chocolate curls.

You may substitute 1/4 cup crème de menthe for the amaretto to make Chocolate Mint Cheesecake. Store the chocolate curls in an airtight container in the freezer until serving time.

Velma Allen, Knoxville, Tennessee

FAT-FREE BROWNIES

Makes 16

> **1 cup sugar**
> **1/2 cup applesauce**
> **1 teaspoon vanilla extract**
> **4 egg whites**
> **2/3 cup flour**
> **1/2 cup baking cocoa**
> **1/8 teaspoon salt**

Combine sugar, applesauce, vanilla extract and egg whites in medium mixer bowl; mix well. Stir in flour, baking cocoa and salt. Spoon into 8x8-inch baking pan sprayed lightly with cooking spray.

Bake at 350 degrees for 25 to 30 minutes or until tester inserted in center comes out nearly clean; do not overbake. Cool and cut into 2-inch squares.

Lauren Howell, Oak Ridge, Tennessee

NO-BAKE SWEET BARS

Makes 18

> **1 1/2 cups chunky natural-style peanut butter**
> **1 cup honey**
> **3/4 cup packed brown sugar**
> **5 cups bran or oat flake cereal**
> **1 cup chopped dried fruit**

Combine peanut butter, honey and brown sugar in large saucepan. Bring to a boil, stirring constantly. Remove from heat; stir in cereal and dried fruit immediately.

Spray 9x13-inch dish with cooking spray. Press mixture evenly into dish. Cool for 15 minutes. Cut into bars.

Bess Hammock, Knoxville, Tennessee

AN EXTRA SLICE

On the afternoon before the Tennessee-South Carolina game early in the 1969-70 season, Coach Mears and his close friend and Number one Vol fan, Knoxville automobile dealer Ken Rice, were taking a walk in downtown Columbia. In one store they spotted some exquisite—and expensive—stuffed gamecocks, symbolic mascots of the South Carolina team.

"I'll tell you what, Ray," said Rice. "If you beat South Carolina tonight, I'll buy one of those gamecocks and give it to you as a souvenir of the win."

Ken thought his money was pretty safe. South Carolina was listed as a 24-point favorite! Tennessee, however, "out-fought and out-rebounded" their bigger rivals from the opening tipoff. With the starting five playing all the way, the Vols won, 55 to 54, in the most startling upset of the season.

Ken Rice very happily reached down into his billfold to pay for the stuffed gamecock. It occupies a place of honor in the Mears home to this day.

SUNDAY BARBECUED CHICKEN AND VEGETABLE SOUP

Serves several

Take your leftover tailgating barbecued chicken and throw it in a big saucepan with a little more of your favorite barbecue sauce, 1 quart of V-8 juice, 2 cans of chicken broth, chopped onions and potatoes, peas and/or butter beans, corn and/or yellow squash, a quarter head of coarsely chopped cabbage and any other veggies you wish (except broccoli). Simmer all morning, remove the bones, add whatever salt and pepper you need and serve with crusty garlic bread and cheese.

Hal J. Daniel III, Greenville, North Carolina

VEGETARIAN SPAGHETTI SAUCE

Serves 6

1 large onion, thinly sliced
3 or 4 cloves of garlic, minced
1 cup finely chopped green bell pepper
3 tablespoons olive oil
3 pounds tomatoes, peeled, seeded
1 tablespoon dried basil
1 tablespoon dried oregano
1 tablespoon red pepper flakes (optional)
1 small carrot, grated or 1 teaspoon sugar
3 tablespoons tomato paste

Sauté onion, garlic and green pepper in heated olive oil in 3-quart saucepan over medium-low heat until tender. Add tomatoes. Simmer until thickened to desired consistency.

Add basil, oregano pepper flakes and carrot. Cook until done to taste. Stir in tomato paste. Serve over spaghetti.

David Ming, Knoxville, Tennessee

Back in the 1960s, Hal Daniel used to prepare soup after the Vol games, using the leftovers from tailgating parties. "Lots of my buddies would come over on Sunday to eat heartily. I still prepare this inexpensive, tasty veggie soup."

BIG ORANGE SCOTTISH SPAGHETTI SAUCE

Serves 8

> 1 tablespoon (about) olive oil
> 1 pound lean ground beef
> 1 onion, chopped
> 1 (6-ounce) can tomato paste
> 3 carrots, chopped
> 3 stalks celery, chopped
> 1 (8-ounce) can mushrooms in butter sauce
> 1 (16-ounce) can tomatoes
> 3 (15-ounce) cans tomato sauce
> Garlic salt and pepper to taste

Heat enough olive oil in saucepan over medium heat to cover bottom of pan. Add ground beef, onion and tomato paste. Cook until ground beef begins to brown, stirring constantly.

Add carrots and celery. Cook for 5 minutes. Add mushrooms and tomatoes. Cook for 3 minutes, stirring constantly. Stir in tomato sauce, garlic salt and pepper.

Simmer for 3 hours. Serve over spaghetti.

Duncan Stewart, Nashville, Tennessee

PRESS BOX MEAT LOAF

Serves 6

   2 or 3 slices stale bread, torn
   1/4 cup milk, warmed
   1 pound ground chuck
   1/3 pound ground pork
   1 small onion, chopped
   2 eggs
   Salt and pepper to taste
   1 (10-ounce) can tomato soup

Soak bread in milk in bowl. Add ground chuck, ground pork, onion, eggs, salt, pepper and 1/3 can soup; mix well. Shape into loaf; place in 6x10-inch baking pan.

Add enough water to remaining soup in can to fill can; mix well. Pour over and around meat loaf.

Bake at 350 degrees for 1 hour.

You may add green pepper and celery to this if you like.

Tom and Kathleen Elam, Union City, Tennessee

Tom Elam (1931, 1934), an attorney in Union City, has served on the UT Board of Trustees and the Athletics Board longer than any other member, having been appointed as a trustee in 1956. The Press Box in Neyland Stadium is named after Colonel Tom and Kathleen Elam. He proudly claims that the University of Tennessee is the most important institution in the state. "I don't think any state is a good one without a good state university. As the state's land grant college, UT has representatives in every county. It reaches in and touches almost every phase of life as we know it today, whether it be planting the corn crop, delivering babies, looking for a cure for cancer or trying to find an answer to the nuclear problem."

In June of 1946, Pat arrived in Knoxville by train as a Yankee bride. "My husband was a student at UT under the GI Bill. Even though I was working, money was tight and we ate a lot of bologna at $.29 a pound."

BOLOGNA SANDWICH SPREAD

Serves 6

8 ounces bologna, ground
1 1/2 cups shredded Cheddar cheese
1 hard-cooked egg, chopped
1/4 cup chopped onion
1/4 cup sweet pickle relish
2 tablespoons prepared mustard
1/2 cup (or more) mayonnaise
Salt and pepper to taste

Combine bologna, cheese, egg, onion, relish, mustard, mayonnaise, salt and pepper in bowl; mix well.

Serve as sandwich spread or as a salad on lettuce or tomatoes.

Pat Shepard, Dickson, Tennessee

Nikki was a Lady Vol basketball player from 1990 to 1994. She holds the school record for the most career-made three-point shots in Lady Vol history, with 103. She received the Gloria Ray Leadership Award in 1993.

SPAM AND RICE

Serves 6

1 (12-ounce) can Spam, diced
1 green bell pepper, chopped
Worcestershire sauce to taste
2 cups cooked rice

Combine Spam, green pepper and Worcestershire sauce in skillet. Cook for 5 minutes over medium heat, stirring constantly.

Add rice and additional Worcestershire sauce. Cook until heated through.

Nikki Caldwell, Oak Ridge, Tennessee

FRIED CHICKEN

Serves 6

Flour
Garlic powder,
  Old Bay
  seasoning,
  seasoned salt
  and pepper
  to taste
1 chicken, cut
  up
Oil for frying
Chopped onion
Chopped
  tomato

Mix flour, garlic powder, Old Bay seasoning, seasoned salt and pepper in bowl. Rinse chicken. Coat with flour mixture. Fry in deep oil in cast-iron skillet until golden brown

Photograph courtesy of *The Orlando Sentinel*

and cooked through; remove chicken to drain. Drain most of the drippings from skillet. Add onion, tomato and desired amount of water to remaining drippings in skillet. Cook until of consistency for gravy. Serve with chicken.

■ This recipe was the favorite of Bridgette's father.

Bridgette Gordon, Como, Italy

Bridgette Gordon is only the second player in Lady Vol basketball history to have her jersey retired. During her four years as a Lady Vol, she captured three All-SEC honors, two Kodak All-America honors and was named MVP of the 1989 NCAA Final Four. In 1988, she led the USA basketball team to a gold medal. She currently plays professional basketball in Como, Italy.

GRAND LAGOON STUFFED FLOUNDER

Serves 10

1 large onion, chopped
2 green bell peppers, chopped
1/2 stalk celery, chopped
4 eggs
1 (16-ounce) package crackers, crushed
11/2 pounds crab claw meat
Juice of 2 lemons
1/2 cup prepared mustard
1/2 cup Worcestershire sauce
2 cups mayonnaise-type salad dressing
2 tablespoons salt
1 tablespoon pepper
5 medium flounder, cleaned
1/2 cup melted butter
3 tablespoons lemon juice

Combine onion, green peppers, celery, eggs, cracker crumbs, crab meat, juice of 2 lemons, mustard, Worcestershire sauce, salad dressing, salt and pepper in bowl; mix well.

Bone flounder by cutting through the middle of the top side and removing bones. Spoon stuffing mixture into cavities. Place in baking dish.

Bake at 350 degrees for 25 minutes, basting with a mixture of the melted butter and 3 tablespoons lemon juice.

The dressing in this recipe may also be used to stuff shrimp.

Sharlyn Bolinger, Knoxville, Tennessee

CURRIED SHRIMP

Serves 6

- 1/4 cup finely chopped onion
- 1/2 cup butter
- 1 large tart apple, peeled, chopped
- 1 cup milk
- 2 chicken bouillon cubes
- 1 cup hot water
- 1 tablespoon flour
- 2 teaspoons curry powder
- 1/2 teaspoon salt
- 11/4 pounds frozen shrimp
- 1 cup rice, cooked

Sauté onion in butter in skillet for 5 minutes. Add apple. Sauté for 5 minutes longer.

Heat milk in saucepan. Stir in bouillon dissolved in hot water. Tilt skillet with sautéed mixture to drain drippings to 1 side. Stir flour, curry powder and salt into drippings. Stir in milk mixture gradually.

Add frozen shrimp. Cook for 10 to 15 minutes or until shrimp are pink and sauce is thickened, stirring occasionally. Serve over rice.

■ When I asked my family—five of them UT graduates—they all gave this as their favorite recipe. They refer to it as green shrimp.

Dell A. Caldwell, Springville, Tennessee

Bob Kesling is Sports Director at Channel 10 in Knoxville, is sideline reporter for Jefferson-Pilot telecasts of SEC football, and is the voice of the Tennessee Lady Vols. He tells the following story: "While at UT, I worked for the Knoxville Sox baseball team in the summertime in the public relations department; Ed Holtz was our general manager. We were in the Southern League playoffs in 1978 and couldn't get to UT's opening football game. Ed had a grill set up in his back yard complete with cinder blocks that stretched about five yards. After the game, the entire Sox team came to Ed's house. We grilled about 200 ears of corn and rooted for Tennessee on TV. The Sox won the Southern League championship that year. So grill more corn!"

KESLING KORN

Serves one and all

Corn—just corn—fresh off the stalk!
Melted butter
Salt to taste

Soak corn in shucks for 20 to 30 minutes. Place on preheated medium-high grill, shucks and all.

Grill for about 5 minutes, turning 1/4 of the way every minute. Remove from grill when shuck is brown all over.

Peel back shuck, dip in butter, season with salt to taste and go at it.

It helps to keep cans of melted butter by the grill to keep the butter warm.

Bob Kesling
Knoxville, Tennessee

206

BIG ORANGE SWEET POTATOES

Serves 4

 2 medium navel oranges
 1 tablespoon butter or margarine
 1 1/2 tablespoons finely chopped pecans
 1 (16-ounce) can sweet potatoes, drained, mashed
 2 tablespoons brown sugar
 1/2 teaspoon pumpkin pie spice
 1/8 teaspoon salt

Cut oranges into halves. Scoop out pulp, reserving 1/4 cup pulp and 3 tablespoons orange juice. Clip and discard orange sections, reserving shells.

Place butter in glass measure. Microwave on High for 35 seconds or until melted. Spread pecans in shallow glass dish. Microwave on High for 2 minutes, stirring after 1 minute.

Combine sweet potatoes, reserved orange pulp, reserved orange juice, butter, pecans, brown sugar, pie spice and salt in bowl; mix well. Spoon into orange shells.

Place stuffed orange shells in shallow glass dish; cover with waxed paper. Microwave on High for 5 minutes.

Kim Newman (1979), Maryville, Tennessee

FIESTA SQUASH CASSEROLE

Serves 12

> 5 or 6 yellow squash, sliced
> 2 or 3 zucchini squash, sliced
> 2 medium onions, sliced
> 16 ounces process cheese
> 3 or 4 jalapeño peppers, finely chopped
> 1 (10-ounce) can cream of mushroom soup
> 1/4 cup picante sauce
> 1 envelope taco seasoning mix
> 2 cups crushed tortilla chips

Cook squash and onions in water to cover in saucepan for 10 minutes or until tender; drain and mash mixture.

Combine cheese, jalapeño peppers, soup, picante sauce and taco seasoning mix in saucepan. Cook over low heat until cheese melts, stirring to mix well. Add squash mixture and half the tortilla chips; mix lightly.

Spoon into greased 9x13-inch baking dish. Top with remaining tortilla chips.

Bake at 350 degrees for 30 minutes or until bubbly and golden brown.

You may freeze this casserole and bake it frozen.

Ann B. Poyner, Liberty, Texas

COTTAGE CHEESE CROQUETTES

Serves 6

    2 cups cottage cheese
    2 cups bread crumbs
    1/2 cup chopped pecans
    1 tablespoon minced onion
    21/2 tablespoons chopped green bell pepper
    1/2 teaspoon paprika
    1/2 teaspoon salt
    1 to 2 tablespoons (about) milk to moisten
    2 eggs
    3 tablespoons milk
    1 cup very fine bread crumbs
    Oil for deep-frying

Combine cottage cheese, 2 cups bread crumbs, pecans, onion, green pepper, paprika and salt in bowl; mix well. Add milk if needed to moisten. Shape into croquettes.

Dip into beaten mixture of eggs and 3 tablespoons milk; coat with 1 cup bread crumbs. Deep-fry in oil until light brown. Serve with cream sauce. You may add a few green peas to the sauce for color and flavor.

Ruth DeFriese, Knoxville, Tennessee

According to Ruth, "Cottage Cheese Croquettes was a very famous recipe of the University Cafeteria in the 1930s, when I worked there during my four under-graduate years and, later, as a dietitian. Many of my tips on food preparation, marketing and storage are from a notebook kept during those days."

AUTUMN FRUIT SALSA

Serves 6

1 cup each chopped apple, pear and plums
1/2 cup thinly sliced green onions
1 tablespoon each lemon juice and cider vinegar
3 tablespoons unsweetened apple juice
1/2 teaspoon ground ginger
1/4 teaspoon each ground coriander and allspice
Crushed red pepper to taste

Combine apple, pear, plums, green onions and lemon juice in bowl; mix gently. Add remaining ingredients; toss lightly. Let stand at room temperature for 1 hour or longer.

Julie Cantrell, Knoxville, Tennessee
Staff, College of Human Ecology

VOLUNTEER JAM

Yields 4 (1/2-pint) jars

7 green bell peppers
2 jalapeño peppers, chopped
11/2 cups each vinegar and apple juice
1 package Sure-Jel
1/2 teaspoon salt
5 cups sugar
Red and yellow food coloring

Purée peppers with vinegar 1/2 at a time in blender or food processor. Combine with apple juice in large bowl. Chill, covered, for 8 hours or longer.

Measure 4 cups of the pepper mixture and combine with Sure-Jel and salt in saucepan. Bring to a rolling boil, stirring constantly. Add sugar. Bring to a boil and boil for 1 minute, stirring constantly. Tint as desired.

Spoon into hot sterilized jars, leaving 1/2 inch headspace; seal with 1-piece lids. Serve with cream cheese on crackers.

Jean H. Bruer, Lewisburg, Tennessee

BIG ORANGE TOMATO SAUCE

Yields 1 gallon

1 gallon ripe or green tomatoes
4 cups sugar
2 cups apple cider vinegar
Seasonings

Peel 1 gallon of ripe or green tomatoes. Add 4 cups of sugar. Pour 2 cups apple cider vinegar over tomatoes. Bring to a boil in a heavy pot; cut heat down. Simmer for 5 minutes for ripe tomatoes or for 10 minutes for green tomatoes or until thickened. Add seasoning as needed and serve as is for **Mild Tomato Sauce**. For **Hot Sauce**, add 1 teaspoon Tabasco sauce. For **Spaghetti Sauce**, add 2 tablespoons basil and 2 tablespoons oregano.

Bob Woodruff, Knoxville, Tennessee

Bob Woodruff wrote this special recipe himself. He was Athletic Director at UT from 1963 to 1985 and oversaw the development of a well-rounded athletic program over that period of time. A Vol letterman himself (1936-1938), he served as head coach at Baylor and Florida and was line coach at Tennessee three different times in 1939, 1941, and 1961 to 1962, before becoming Athletic Director. He is a member of the Tennessee and Georgia Halls of Fame.

211

CHOCOLATE CRINKLE COOKIES

Makes 50

1/2 cup corn oil
2 cups sugar
4 (1-ounce) squares unsweetened chocolate, melted
4 eggs
2 cups flour
2 teaspoons baking powder
1/2 teaspoon salt
2 teaspoons vanilla extract
1 cup confectioners' sugar

Combine corn oil, sugar and melted chocolate in bowl. Beat in eggs 1 at a time. Add flour, baking powder, salt and vanilla; mix well. Chill for 8 hours or longer.

Shape into 1-inch balls and coat with confectioners' sugar. Place on greased baking sheet.

Bake at 350 degrees for 10 minutes. Remove to wire rack to cool completely.

Betty M. Gill, Knoxville, Tennessee

UT

Betty was the 1988-1989 President of the National Alumni Association, and is currently serving on the Athletics Board. These cookies were sent to campus many times during exam week for their four sons. They are a favorite at the Gill house, especially during the holidays.

'NILLA ORANGE BALLS

Makes 40

1 (16-ounce) package vanilla wafers, finely crushed
1/2 cup melted margarine
1/4 cup thawed frozen orange juice concentrate
1 cup confectioners' sugar
1/2 cup chopped pecans
1 cup confectioners' sugar

Combine cookie crumbs, margarine, orange juice concentrate, 1 cup confectioners' sugar and pecans in bowl; mix well. Shape into balls.

Roll in additional confectioners' sugar. The flavor improves if the orange balls are allowed to stand for at least 24 hours. Store in airtight container.

Ned McWherter, Dresden, Tennessee

Ned McWherter served as the 46th Governor of Tennessee from 1986 to 1994. When he campaigned for office, one of his offhand comments to emphasize his vast political experience was "Swear me in at 10 o'clock in the morning, give me a cup of coffee and four vanilla wafers, and I'll be ready to go to work." This remark led to a flurry of publicity about his preference for vanilla wafers, including an article in *People* magazine with a full-page photograph of the governor in front of the State Capitol Building holding a box of 'Nilla Wafers. This recipe was sent to Governor McWherter by Susan Rosen, a fifth-grade student in Bartlett, Tennessee, in 1987.

LEMON MERINGUE PIE

Serves 8

Pat McGlothin pitched for the Vols baseball team from 1939 to 1941, and played professionally in the Brooklyn Dodgers organization from 1941 to 1953. He is now with the Mutual Insurance Agency in Knoxville. His assessment of Lemon Meringue Pie: "The only thing better than this is to pitch a no-hitter."

1 1/2 cups sugar
3 tablespoons cornstarch
3 tablespoons flour
Salt to taste
1 1/2 cups hot water
3 egg yolks, slightly beaten
1/2 teaspoon grated lemon rind
2 tablespoons butter or margarine
1/3 cup lemon juice
1 baked (9-inch) pie shell
3 egg whites
1 teaspoon lemon juice
6 tablespoons sugar

Mix 1 1/2 cups sugar, cornstarch, flour and salt in saucepan. Blend in hot water gradually. Bring to a boil over high heat, stirring constantly; reduce heat to medium. Cook for 8 minutes longer, stirring constantly.

Stir a small amount of hot mixture into egg yolks; stir egg yolks into hot mixture. Bring to a boil over high heat, stirring constantly. Reduce heat to low. Cook for 4 minutes, stirring constantly; remove from heat.

Stir in lemon rind and butter. Add 1/3 cup lemon juice gradually. Place plastic wrap directly on surface of custard; let stand for 1 hour or until cool. Spoon into pie shell.

Beat egg whites with 1 teaspoon lemon juice in mixer bowl until soft peaks form. Add 6 tablespoons sugar gradually, beating constantly until stiff peaks form and sugar dissolves.

Spread meringue over pie filling, sealing to edge. Bake at 350 degrees for 12 to 15 minutes or until golden brown. Cool completely before serving.

Pat McGlothin, Knoxville, Tennessee

THE LAST SLICE

One Tennessee fan who set a record for Volunteering is Duncan Stewart. In September of 1988, Tennessee's football season got off to its worst start in 26 years with a record of 0-4. On September 20, Duncan, a Nashville radio talk show host for 98WSIX, set up housekeeping on the platform of a bright orange "Go Big Orange" billboard located above Interstate 40. He vowed to stay there until the Vols won a game.

The housekeeping arrangement included a four-foot-wide ledge about 40 feet above the ground. The radio station furnished him with telephones for his evening call-in show. Comforts included a lean-to with a mattress, a reading light, a cooler, food from a local McDonald's and a portable toilet at the base of the billboard.

On September 21, Stewart was quoted in the Nashville newspaper, The Tennessean as saying "I've always been a Tennessee fan. Now I've got an extra reason to pull for them. I don't wanna spend Thanksgiving up here," Fortunately for him, he didn't have to. He was able to come down from his post on October 22, when UT defeated Memphis State.

EASY APPLE DUMPLINGS

Serves 8

1 (8-count) can crescent dinner rolls
2 Granny Smith apples, cut into quarters
1 cup orange juice
1 cup melted margarine
1 cup sugar
1 quart vanilla ice cream

Separate roll dough into 8 triangles. Roll as thin as possible on floured surface. Cut each apple quarter into thin slices, retaining shape of quarter. Place 1 apple quarter in middle of each dough triangle. Pull sides up to enclose apple and pinch together. Place in 9x13-inch baking pan.

Combine orange juice, margarine and sugar in bowl; mix well. Pour over dumplings.

Bake at 400 degrees for 20 to 25 minutes or until browned. Top with ice cream.

Roger Conner, Nashville, Tennessee
Becky Hartman, Knoxville, Tennessee

Roger Conner reports that the weekend of November 9, 1991, was undoubtedly his most memorable; first, because the Vols pulled off the "Miracle at South Bend", defeating Notre Dame in a 35 to 34 comeback victory, and second, because his son Dillon was born the next morning. "His first few minutes in the world were spent making a video with the headlines of the sports section as a backdrop. My wife Melanie had to tolerate me and my two older sons watching the replay of the game only a few minutes after Dillon was born. The perfect end to the perfect day!"

217

APPLE PUDDING SOUFFLE

Serves 8

1 cup chopped tart apples
1/4 cup butter
3 cups bread cubes
2 cups scalded milk
1/2 cup sugar
1/2 cup raisins
1 teaspoon grated lemon rind
1 teaspoon vanilla extract
1/4 teaspoon salt
3 egg yolks, beaten
3 egg whites
1/4 teaspoon nutmeg

Sauté apples in butter in skillet until tender but not brown. Stir in bread cubes. Cook until light brown. Remove from heat.

Add milk, sugar, raisins, lemon rind, vanilla, salt and egg yolks; mix well. Beat egg whites in mixer bowl until soft peaks form. Fold into apple mixture. Spoon into 3-quart casserole. Sprinkle with nutmeg. Set in larger pan of hot water.

Bake at 350 degrees for 45 minutes.

Mary Ann Harding, Germantown, Tennessee

BANANA PUDDING

Serves 12

1 (16-ounce) package vanilla wafers
6 bananas, sliced
1 cup sugar
3 tablespoons cornstarch
3 1/2 cups milk
3 egg yolks, slightly beaten
3 tablespoons butter
1 teaspoon vanilla extract

Alternate layers of vanilla wafers and bananas in 2-quart baking dish, beginning and ending with vanilla wafers.

Combine sugar, cornstarch, milk and egg yolks in saucepan. Bring to a slow boil. Cook over medium heat until thickened. Beat in butter and vanilla. Pour cooled pudding over layers. Serve with whipped topping.

Doug Atkins, Knoxville, Tennessee

Doug Atkins came to UT from Humbolt and was an All-America selection in 1952. He played professionally for the Cleveland Browns, the Chicago Bears, and the New Orleans Saints between 1953 and 1969. He is a member of the College and Pro Football Halls of Fame, the only Vol so honored in both Halls. He was named SEC Player of the Quarter Century (1950 to 1974) in a poll of sports writers by the Birmingham Quarterback Club. His best memory at UT is of winning the 1951 National Football Championship.

BLUEBERRY PIZZA

Serves 12

- 1 (2-layer) package white cake mix
- 1 cup quick-cooking oats
- 6 tablespoons butter
- 1 egg
- 1 (21-ounce) can blueberry pie filling
- 1/4 cup quick-cooking oats
- 2 tablespoons butter
- 1/2 cup chopped pecans
- 1/4 cup packed brown sugar
- 1/2 teaspoon cinnamon

Combine cake mix, 1 cup oats and 6 tablespoons butter in mixer bowl; beat at low speed until crumbly. Remove and set aside 1 cup crumbs. Stir egg into remaining crumbs. Press into greased 9x13-inch baking pan.

Bake at 350 degrees for 12 minutes. Spread with pie filling.

Combine reserved crumbs, 1/4 cup oats, 2 tablespoons butter, pecans, brown sugar and cinnamon in bowl; mix well. Sprinkle over pie filling.

Bake at 350 degrees for 15 to 20 minutes longer or until light golden brown. Cool completely. Cut into squares. Serve with whipped topping.

Eddie White, Mt. Juliet, Tennessee

LEMON CHIFFON CHEESECAKE

Serves 12

1 (12-ounce) can evaporated milk
2 cups graham cracker crumbs
1 tablespoon sugar
1/2 cup melted butter
1 (3-ounce) package lemon gelatin
1 cup boiling water
8 ounces cream cheese, softened
1 cup sugar
6 tablespoons lemon juice

Chill evaporated milk in refrigerator for 24 hours and in freezer for 15 minutes.

Mix crumbs with 1 tablespoon sugar in bowl. Stir in melted butter. Pat into 9x13-inch dish.

Dissolve gelatin in boiling water. Chill until of consistency of honey. Beat cream cheese and 1 cup sugar in mixer bowl until light and fluffy. Stir in gelatin mixture. Add lemon juice; mix well.

Beat evaporated milk until stiff peaks form. Fold into filling. Pour into crust. Chill until serving time.

You may reserve a small amount of crumb mixture to sprinkle over top of cheesecake.

■ This recipe is from my aunt. I have enjoyed sharing it, as sharing is one of the joys of life, whether it be recipes, flowers, laughter or anything else.

Mary Jane Coomes, Allons, Tennessee

AMARETTO CAKE

Serves 16

1 cup butter, softened
2¹/₂ cups sugar
6 eggs
1 cup sour cream
2 teaspoons almond extract
1 teaspoon each lemon, orange and vanilla extract
¹/₂ teaspoon salt
¹/₄ teaspoon baking soda
3 cups cake flour
¹/₄ cup amaretto
1 (10-ounce) jar orange marmalade
¹/₄ cup amaretto
¹/₂ (5-ounce) jar apricot preserves
1 cup chopped toasted almonds

Cream butter and sugar in mixer bowl until light and fluffy. Add eggs 1 at a time, beating well after each addition. Add sour cream and almond extract; beat well. Add remaining flavorings, salt, baking soda and flour gradually, beating well after each addition. Beat in ¹/₄ cup amaretto. Pour into greased bundt pan.

Bake at 325 degrees for 1 hour and 15 minutes or until cake tests done. Cool in pan for 10 minutes. Invert onto serving plate.

Combine marmalade, ¹/₄ cup amaretto and preserves in saucepan. Cook until marmalade and preserves are melted, stirring to mix well. Drizzle over cooled cake. Sprinkle with almonds.

Ellene Everhart, Mt. Juliet, Tennessee

CARROT CAKES

Serves 16

2 cups sugar
3 cups flour
1 teaspoon baking soda
1/2 teaspoon salt
1 teaspoon cinnamon
2 cups coarsely grated carrots
11/2 cups vegetable oil
2 eggs, beaten
1 cup chopped pecans
1 cup drained crushed pineapple
1 teaspoon vanilla extract
1 teaspoon lemon extract
1/2 teaspoon almond extract

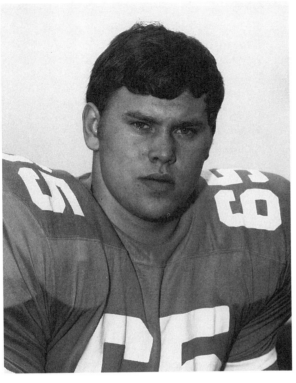

Phillip Fulmer (1972) played offensive guard at UT from 1969 to 1971. He was named head football coach in 1992 after having served as an assistant coach since 1980. He and Vicky think that carrots always add a touch of orange to prepared foods, which, of course, brings to mind tailgate foods and Vol parties. "Add a little orange luck to your next Big Orange party with this delicious carrot cake. Go, Vols!"

Combine sugar, flour, baking soda, salt and cinnamon in bowl; mix well. Add carrots, oil and eggs; beat well. Stir in pecans, pineapple and flavorings. Pour into 2 or 3 oiled and floured small loaf pans.

Bake at 350 degrees for 1 hour. Spread with favorite cream cheese frosting.

Phillip and Vicky Fulmer, Maryville, Tennessee

223

CHOCOLATE-COVERED CHERRY CAKE

Serves 15

> 1 (2-layer) package Swiss chocolate cake mix
> 1 tablespoon flour
> 1 (21-ounce) can cherry pie filling
> 2 eggs
> 1/2 cup milk
> 1 cup sugar
> 5 to 6 tablespoons butter
> 2 cups milk chocolate chips

Combine cake mix and flour in bowl; mix well. Stir in pie filling and eggs. Pour into greased and floured 9x13-inch cake pan.

Bake at 350 degrees for 35 to 40 minutes or until tester comes out clean.

Combine milk, sugar and butter in saucepan. Bring to a boil. Simmer for 1 minute. Add chocolate chips. Cook until melted, stirring constantly. Pour over hot cake.

Ruth Garland, Rutledge, Tennessee

TRIPLE CHOCOLATE CAKE

Serves 15

> 1 (4-ounce) package chocolate pie filling mix
> 1 (2-layer) package chocolate cake mix
> 1 cup chocolate chips
> 1 cup pecans

Prepare pie filling using package directions. Combine with cake mix in bowl; mix well. Pour into greased 11x13-inch cake pan. Top with chocolate chips and pecans.

Bake at 350 degrees for 30 minutes.

■ This cake, which needs no frosting, is great for picnics or tailgate parties.

Ava H. Collett, Stewart, Tennessee

SMOKEY'S MISSISSIPPI MUD CAKE

Serves 24

2 cups self-rising flour
2/3 cup baking cocoa
2 cups sugar
1 cup margarine, softened
4 eggs
1 teaspoon vanilla extract
1 (10-ounce) package miniature marshmallows
1/2 cup butter, softened
1/4 cup baking cocoa
1/8 teaspoon salt
1 (1-pound) package confectioners' sugar
1/4 cup (or more) milk
1 teaspoon vanilla extract

Sift flour with 2/3 cup cocoa. Cream sugar with margarine in mixer bowl until light and fluffy. Add eggs 1 at a time, beating well after each addition. Add flour mixture to creamed mixture gradually, beating well after each addition. Beat in 1 teaspoon vanilla. Spoon into greased 8x12-inch cake pan. Bake at 300 degrees for 20 minutes. Cover top of cake with marshmallows. Bake for 5 minutes longer. Cool in pan.

Combine cup butter, 1/4 cup cocoa and salt in bowl; mix well. Stir in confectioners' sugar. Add milk until of spreading consistency. Beat in 1 teaspoon vanilla. Spread over cooled cake.

You may add 2 cups chopped pecans to cake.

Michelle Foster, Lebanon, Tennessee

TIME-SAVER CHOCOLATE CAKE

Serves 15

2 cups flour
2 cups sugar
1/2 cup butter or margarine
1/4 cup baking cocoa
1/2 cup shortening
1 cup water
2 eggs
1 teaspoon cinnamon
1 teaspoon vanilla extract
1/2 cup buttermilk
1 teaspoon baking soda
Buttermilk Frosting

Sift flour and sugar into large bowl and set aside.

Combine butter, baking cocoa, shortening and water in saucepan. Bring to a boil over low heat, stirring to mix well. Cool slightly. Pour over flour mixture; mix well.

Add eggs, cinnamon, vanilla and mixture of buttermilk and baking soda; mix well. Spoon into greased 9x13-inch cake pan.

Bake at 375 degrees for 45 minutes or until cake springs back when lightly touched. Cool on wire rack. Frost with Buttermilk Frosting.

Buttermilk Frosting

1 cup packed brown sugar
1/2 cup butter or margarine
1/2 teaspoon vanilla extract
1/2 cup buttermilk
1/2 teaspoon baking soda

Combine brown sugar, butter, vanilla and mixture of buttermilk and baking soda in saucepan. Cook to soft-ball stage over low heat. Beat until of spreading consistency.

Nancy and Jimmy Walls, Knoxville, Tennessee

UT

Jimmy Walls was a much-loved and respected professor of geology who taught at UT between 1929 and 1980. He also served as Vol golf coach during his time on the Hill. He loved teaching the introductory course in geology and was one of the favorite professors of Tennessee alumni.

CHOCOLATE SHEET CAKE

Serves 15

2 cups sugar
2 cups flour
1/2 cup margarine
1/2 cup shortening
1/4 cup baking cocoa
1 cup water
1/2 cup buttermilk
2 eggs, slightly beaten
1 teaspoon baking soda
1 teaspoon instant coffee
1 teaspoon vanilla extract
Sheet Cake Frosting

Sift sugar and flour into large bowl. Combine margarine, shortening, baking cocoa and water in saucepan; mix well. Bring to a boil. Pour over flour mixture; mix well. Add buttermilk, eggs, baking soda, coffee granules and vanilla; mix well. Pour into greased and floured 11x16-inch cake pan.

Bake at 400 degrees for 20 to 25 minutes or until cake tests done. Spread hot cake with Sheet Cake Frosting.

Sheet Cake Frosting

1/2 cup margarine
1/4 cup baking cocoa
6 tablespoons milk
1 (1-pound) package confectioners' sugar
1 teaspoon vanilla extract
1 cup chopped pecans

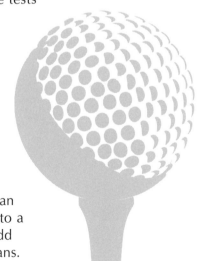

Combine margarine, baking cocoa and milk in saucepan about 5 minutes before cake is through baking. Bring to a boil; simmer until margarine and cocoa are melted. Add confectioners' sugar and vanilla; beat well. Stir in pecans.

Norma and Jim Harris, Knoxville, Tennessee

CHOCOLATE PEPPERMINT LOG

Serves 12

4 egg whites
1/2 cup sugar
4 egg yolks
1 teaspoon vanilla extract
1/3 cup sugar
1/3 cup baking cocoa
1/2 cup flour
1/2 teaspoon baking powder
1/4 teaspoon baking soda
1/8 teaspoon salt
1/3 cup water
Peppermint Filling
Chocolate Log Glaze

Beat egg whites in mixer bowl until foamy. Add 1/2 cup sugar gradually, beating until stiff peaks form; set aside.

Beat egg yolks with vanilla at high speed in mixer bowl for 3 minutes. Add 1/3 cup sugar gradually, beating constantly. Beat for 2 minutes longer. Mix baking cocoa, flour, baking powder, baking soda and salt in bowl. Add to egg yolk mixture alternately with water, beating well after each addition. Fold into egg whites. Spread in foil-lined 10x15-inch cake pan.

Bake at 375 degrees for 12 to 15 minutes or until top springs back when lightly touched. Invert onto towel sprinkled with confectioners' sugar. Remove foil carefully. Roll cake in towel starting from narrow end. Cool on wire rack.

Unroll cake; remove towel. Spread with Peppermint Filling; reroll cake. Drizzle with Chocolate Log Glaze. Chill until serving time.

■ I have had this recipe for a very long time. It is time consuming, but worth the trouble in the end. At Christmas, I decorate it with "holly" made from mint leaves or green gum drops and cherries.

(continued)

Peppermint Filling

1 cup whipping cream
1/4 cup confectioners' sugar
1/4 cup finely crushed peppermint candy or 1/2 teaspoon
   mint extract
Several drops of red food coloring (optional)

Beat whipping cream in mixer bowl until slightly thickened.
Add confectioners' sugar and crushed candy; beat until stiff.
Tint as desired.

Chocolate Log Glaze

2 tablespoons butter
2 tablespoons baking cocoa
2 tablespoons water
1 cup confectioners' sugar
1/2 teaspoon vanilla extract

Melt butter over low heat in saucepan. Add baking cocoa and
water. Cook just until thickened, stirring constantly; do not boil.
Cool slightly. Blend in confectioners' sugar and vanilla.

Mary Jane Coomes, Allons, Tennessee

SOUTHERN WHITE CHOCOLATE CAKE

Serves 16

2 1/2 cups cake flour
1 teaspoon baking powder
1/4 teaspoon salt
1 cup butter, softened
2 cups sugar
4 ounces white chocolate bark, melted
4 eggs
1 cup buttermilk
1 cup finely chopped pecans
1 (3-ounce) can flaked coconut
1/2 teaspoon coconut extract
1/2 teaspoon almond extract
White Chocolate Frosting

Sift flour, baking powder and salt together. Cream butter and sugar in mixer bowl until light and fluffy. Stir in melted white chocolate. Add eggs 1 at a time, beating for 1 minute after each addition. Add flour mixture and buttermilk alternately to creamed mixture, beating well after each addition. Stir in pecans, coconut and flavorings. Pour into greased and floured bundt pan.

Bake at 350 degrees for 1 hour or until cake tests done. Cool in pan for several minutes. Invert onto serving plate. Spread top and side of cake with White Chocolate Frosting.

■ Many thanks to Mattie Sue Ragsdale of Brentwood; this is the recipe for one of her famous and elegant cakes.

(continued)

Ann's husband George says the Nashville Area Alumni picnic has come a long way from the 1950's, when he graduated from UT law school. They could have gathered in a back yard then, but now they fill up an armory!

White Chocolate Frosting

1 cup sugar
1/2 cup butter
4 ounces white chocolate bark
1/4 cup evaporated milk
1 tablespoon light corn syrup
1/8 teaspoon salt
1/4 teaspoon each coconut extract and almond extract
12 miniature marshmallows

Combine sugar, butter, chocolate, evaporated milk, corn syrup, salt and flavorings in saucepan; mix well. Set aside for 1 hour, stirring occasionally.

Cook over medium heat to soft-ball stage. Stir in marshmallows. Let stand until cool. Beat until of spreading consistency.

Ann Harsh Linebaugh, Brentwood, Tennessee

COCONUT CAKE

Serves 12

1 (2-layer) package butter-recipe white or yellow cake mix
2 cups sugar
2 cups sour cream
8 ounces whipped topping
1 (12-ounce) package frozen fresh coconut

Prepare and bake cake mix using package directions for two 8-inch round cake pans. Cut layers into halves horizontally.

Mix sugar with sour cream in bowl; reserve 1 cup for frosting. Spread remaining sour cream mixture between layers of cake, stacking cut side up on serving plate.

Mix reserved sour cream mixture with whipped topping. Spread over top and side of cake. Sprinkle with coconut. Garnish with cherries or Big Orange slices. Store in refrigerator for 8 hours or longer before serving.

Pam Baucom, Franklin, Tennessee

Pam's greatest memory of UT is watching for her future husband, Tom, to run through the Big T before a football game in the late '60s. "He played for UT on a football scholarship in '67, '68 and '69; his whole family was so proud! The excitement that builds before this event is almost indescribable, even today. I will always be grateful for what the University of Tennessee has meant for my entire family."

COMPANY COCONUT CAKE

Serves 12

> **3 eggs**
> **3/4 cup vegetable oil**
> **1 cup sour cream**
> **1 (8-ounce) can cream of coconut**
> **1/2 teaspoon vanilla extract**
> **1 (2-layer) package white cake mix**
> **Coconut Cream Cheese Frosting**

Beat eggs in mixer bowl until light. Add oil, sour cream and cream of coconut, beating well after each addition. Stir in vanilla. Add cake mix, beating at low speed until blended. Beat at high speed for 2 minutes. Pour into 3 greased and floured 8-inch cake pans.

Bake at 325 degrees for 35 to 45 minutes or until layers test done. Cool in pans for several minutes. Remove to wire racks to cool completely. Spread Coconut Cream Cheese Frosting between layers and over top and side of cake.

Coconut Cream Cheese Frosting

> **1/2 cup margarine, softened**
> **8 ounces cream cheese, softened**
> **1 teaspoon vanilla extract**
> **1 (1-pound) package confectioners' sugar**
> **1 (7-ounce) package coconut**

Cream margarine and cream cheese in mixer bowl until light and fluffy. Beat in vanilla. Add confectioners' sugar gradually, beating well after each addition. Stir in coconut.

Phyllis L. Bogle, Memphis, Tennessee

GRAND MARNIER CAKE

Serves 16

    1 cup butter or margarine, softened
    1 cup sugar
    3 egg yolks
    1 tablespoon Grand Marnier
    2 cups flour
    1 teaspoon baking powder
    1 teaspoon baking soda
    1 1/4 cups sour cream
    Grated zest of 1 orange
    1 cup chopped pecans, toasted
    3 egg whites, stiffly beaten
    1/2 cup sugar
    1 cup orange juice
    1/3 cup Grand Marnier
    1/2 cup slivered almonds

Cream butter and 1 cup sugar in mixer bowl until light and fluffy. Add egg yolks 1 at a time, beating well after each addition. Beat in 1 tablespoon Grand Marnier.

Add sifted mixture of flour, baking powder and baking soda alternately with sour cream, beating well after each addition. Stir in orange zest and pecans. Fold in egg whites. Spoon into greased 10-cup bundt pan.

Bake at 350 degrees for 50 minutes. Cool in pan. Invert onto serving platter. Drizzle with mixture of 1/2 cup sugar, orange juice and 1/3 cup Grand Marnier just before serving. Sprinkle with almonds.

Jennifer Webb, Knoxville, Tennessee

PEACH UPSIDE-DOWN CAKE

Serves 8

1/2 cup peach juice
1/2 cup packed brown sugar
1/4 cup sugar
2 tablespoons light corn syrup
1 (16-ounce) can sliced peaches, drained
11/4 cups sifted cake flour
1 teaspoon baking powder
1/4 teaspoon salt
1/4 cup butter, softened
2/3 cup sugar
2 eggs
1/2 teaspoon vanilla extract
1/3 cup milk

Bring peach juice, brown sugar, 1/4 cup sugar and corn syrup to a boil in saucepan; mix well. Boil over medium heat to 230 to 234 degrees on candy thermometer, spun-thread stage. Pour into 9-inch cake pan or skillet. Arrange peaches in syrup.

Sift cake flour, baking powder and salt together 3 times. Cream butter in mixer bowl until light and fluffy. Beat in 2/3 cup sugar until blended. Add eggs 1 at a time, beating well after each addition. Stir in vanilla. Add dry ingredients alternately with milk, beating well after each addition. Pour over peaches.

Bake at 350 degrees for 35 minutes. Cool in pan for 10 minutes. Invert onto serving platter.

Mildred L. Winningham, Crossville, Tennessee

BUTTERSCOTCH ICEBOX COOKIES

Makes 96

4 cups sifted flour
1 teaspoon (scant) baking soda
1 teaspoon cream of tartar
1 teaspoon salt
1/2 cup butter or margarine, softened
1/2 cup shortening
1 cup packed brown sugar
1 cup sugar
2 eggs
1 1/2 teaspoons vanilla extract
1 cup chopped pecans

Sift flour, baking soda, cream of tartar and salt together.

Cream butter, shortening, brown sugar and sugar in mixer bowl until light and fluffy. Add eggs, beating until blended. Beat in vanilla. Stir in dry ingredients and pecans.

Shape dough into three 2-inch logs; wrap with waxed paper. Chill for several hours or until firm. Cut into 1/8-inch slices. Arrange on nonstick cookie sheet.

Bake at 400 degrees for 7 minutes or until light brown. Remove to wire rack to cool completely.

■ My grandmother always baked these for Thanksgiving and Christmas holidays, and they bring back happy memories of my past.

John and Barbara Ward, Knoxville, Tennessee

TENNESSEE GOURMET CHOCOLATE CHIP COOKIES

Makes 130

5 cups rolled oats
4 cups flour
2 teaspoons baking soda
2 teaspoons baking powder
2 teaspoons salt
2 cups margarine, softened
2 cups packed brown sugar
2 cups sugar
4 eggs
2 teaspoons vanilla extract
4 cups milk chocolate chips
6 (1-ounce) chocolate candy bars, broken into bite-size pieces

Process oats in blender or food processor for 1 minute or until of powdery consistency. Combine with flour, baking soda, baking powder and salt in bowl; mix well.

Cream margarine, brown sugar and sugar in mixer bowl until light and fluffy. Beat in eggs and vanilla until blended. Add oat mixture; mix well. Stir in chocolate chips and candy pieces. Shape into balls. Arrange on nonstick cookie sheet.

Bake at 350 degrees for 15 minutes. Remove to wire rack to cool completely.

Patsy Green, Hermitage, Tennessee

EASY CHOCOLATE CHIP COOKIES

Makes 36

2 eggs
1/3 cup shortening
1 (2-layer) package butter cake mix
1 teaspoon vanilla extract
2 cups semisweet chocolate chips

Combine eggs and shortening in bowl; mix well. Add cake mix gradually, mixing well after each addition. Stir in vanilla and chocolate chips.

Drop by teaspoonfuls onto ungreased cookie sheet.

Bake at 325 degrees for 10 minutes. Cool on wire rack.

Betty Colvett Neilson, Huron, Tennessee

FRUIT COOKIES

Makes 24

1 cup butter, softened
1 cup sugar
2 tablespoons milk
1 teaspoon vanilla or rum extract
2 1/2 cups flour, sifted
3/4 cup finely chopped candied cherries
1/2 cup each chopped pecans and coconut

Cream butter and sugar in mixer bowl until light and fluffy. Add milk, vanilla and flour, stirring until blended. Stir in cherries and pecans; mix well. Shape into logs; roll in coconut.

Chill, wrapped in waxed paper, for 12 hours. Cut into 1/2-inch slices. Arrange on greased cookie sheet.

Bake at 375 degrees for 12 minutes. Remove to wire rack to cool.

You may substitute any candied fruit for the cherries. Store the dough in the refrigerator for 2 to 3 weeks, and bake as desired.

Lela and Mike Miller, Kingsport, Tennessee

Betty made many batches of these cookies while working on her graduate degree in textiles and clothing at the University of Tennessee in Knoxville. "This recipe was perfect because it did not require the use of an electric mixer to mix the dough. (I didn't even own a mixer and neither did my apartment mate.) We used all varieties of cake mixes as well as different flavored chips. A very versatile cookie recipe for two single girls on a limited budget."

237

QUICK PEANUT BUTTER COOKIES

Makes 36

1 cup corn syrup
1 cup sugar
1 cup peanut butter
6 cups cornflakes

Combine corn syrup and sugar in saucepan; mix well. Cook over medium heat until sugar dissolves, stirring constantly. Stir in peanut butter.

Pour peanut butter mixture over cornflakes in bowl, tossing to coat. Drop by teaspoonfuls onto waxed paper. Let stand until cool.

Nancy Rucker, Ashland City, Tennessee

The first time Nancy made these cookies she was a student at The University of Tennessee in Chattanooga. These cookies are great for casual parties or any occasion. Nancy is now employed by the University of Tennessee Agricultural Extension Service and is still making these cookies.

EASY PEANUT BUTTER BLOSSOM COOKIES

Makes 60

1 (14-ounce) can sweetened condensed milk
3/4 cup peanut butter
2 cups baking mix
1 teaspoon vanilla extract
1 cup sugar
60 chocolate candy kisses

Beat condensed milk and peanut butter in mixer bowl until smooth. Add baking mix and vanilla; mix well.

Shape dough into 1-inch balls; roll in sugar. Place 2 inches apart on ungreased cookie sheet.

Bake at 375 degrees for 6 to 8 minutes or until light brown. Press 1 candy kiss into center of each hot cookie. Remove to wire rack to cool completely.

Dale Bradley, Knoxville, Tennessee

PEANUT BUTTER TEMPTATIONS

Makes 48

1/2 cup butter, softened
1/2 cup peanut butter
1/2 cup sugar
1/2 cup packed brown sugar
1 egg
1/2 teaspoon vanilla extract
11/4 cups flour
3/4 teaspoon baking soda
1/2 teaspoon salt
48 miniature peanut butter cups

Cream butter, peanut butter, sugar, brown sugar, egg and vanilla in mixer bowl until light and fluffy. Stir in mixture of flour, baking soda and salt; mix well.

Shape dough into 1-inch balls. Press evenly over bottom and sides of miniature muffin cups.

Bake at 350 degrees for 11 minutes. Press 1 peanut butter cup into center of each muffin cup. Let stand until cool.

■ For peanut butter-loving fans of the Big Orange, this recipe travels well across I-40 to Knoxville on football weekends. It has become a staple around the holidays, especially for New Year's Day Bowl parties!

Janet E. Cordell, Dickson, Tennessee

AMBER PIE

Serves 6

> 1 cup sugar
> 2 tablespoons cornstarch
> 2 cups milk
> 2 egg yolks, beaten
> 1/3 cup margarine
> 1/2 cup raisins
> 1/2 teaspoon cinnamon
> 1/2 teaspoon nutmeg
> 1/2 teaspoon mace
> 1/2 teaspoon allspice
> 1 teaspoon vinegar
> 1 baked (9-inch) pie shell
> 2 egg whites
> 1/8 teaspoon cream of tartar
> 1/4 cup sugar
> 1/2 teaspoon vanilla extract

Combine 1 cup sugar and cornstarch in saucepan; mix well. Stir in milk gradually. Cook over medium-low heat just until mixture begins to thicken, stirring constantly.

Stir a small amount of hot mixture into egg yolks; stir egg yolks into hot mixture. Cook until thickened, stirring constantly. Remove from heat. Stir in margarine, raisins, cinnamon, nutmeg, mace, allspice and vinegar. Spoon into pie shell.

Beat egg whites with cream of tartar in mixer bowl until foamy. Add 1/4 cup sugar gradually, beating constantly until stiff peaks form. Beat in vanilla. Spread over filling, sealing to edge.

Bake at 400 degrees for 8 minutes or until light brown.

■ This recipe was given to me by my mother-in-law in 1946. It was one of her favorites.

Ann T. Wagster, Jackson, Tennessee

BOB'S FAVORITE APPLE PIE

Serves 6

- 1/2 to 2/3 cup sugar
- 1/2 teaspoon cinnamon
- 1/2 teaspoon nutmeg
- 2 teaspoons flour
- 6 large Granny Smith apples, sliced
- 1 unbaked (9-inch) deep-dish pie shell
- 1/2 cup butter, softened
- 1/2 cup packed brown sugar
- 1 cup flour

Combine sugar, cinnamon, nutmeg and 2 teaspoons flour in bowl; mix well. Add apples, tossing to coat. Spread evenly over bottom of pie shell.

Combine butter and brown sugar in bowl, stirring with fork until mixed. Add 1 cup flour, stirring until crumbly. Sprinkle over apples.

Bake at 450 degrees for 15 minutes. Reduce temperature to 350 degrees. Bake until bubbly and golden brown.

You may use any type of apple in this recipe.

Jane D. Johnson
Glendale, Ohio

Jane is married to Bob Johnson who was captain of the 1967 Tennessee football team. He was named All-America in 1966-67 and Academic All-America in 1967. He was the number one draft choice of the Cincinnati Bengals in 1968 and played for the Bengals for 12 seasons. He is now president of Imperial Adhesives, Inc. in Cincinnati. Jane writes that one of her best memories is of the reunion of the 1967 SEC Championship Team. The reunion was attended by most of the team and coaches. "It was great to see all our old friends and teammates."

GRANNY'S BUTTERSCOTCH PIE

Serves 6

1 cup packed brown sugar
1/4 cup flour
3 tablespoons butter
1/4 teaspoon salt
2 1/4 cups milk, scalded
4 egg yolks
1 teaspoon vanilla extract
1 baked (9-inch) pie shell
3 egg whites
1/4 teaspoon cream of tartar
1/4 cup sugar
1 teaspoon vanilla extract

Combine brown sugar, flour, butter and salt in double boiler. Cook over hot water until blended, stirring constantly. Stir in milk.

Beat egg yolks in bowl until lemon-colored. Pour small amount of hot milk mixture into egg yolks, beating until blended. Stir egg yolk mixture into milk mixture.

Cook until slightly thickened, stirring constantly. Remove from heat. Beat until cool. Stir in 1 teaspoon vanilla. Pour into pie shell.

Beat egg whites in mixer bowl until frothy. Add cream of tartar. Beat until stiff peaks form. Beat in 1/4 cup sugar gradually. Stir in 1 teaspoon vanilla. Spread over filling, sealing to edge.

Bake at 325 degrees for 10 to 15 minutes or until light brown.

Bob Bell, Springfield, Tennessee

UT

Bob Bell has been Sports Director at WLAC Radio in Nashville since 1987. He worked with Channel 2 in Nashville for 20 years prior to his employment at WLAC. He has been affiliated with the Vol Network and has done pay-per-view games for Host Communications.

MOCHA FUDGE PIE

Serves 8

2 teaspoons instant coffee granules
1/3 cup hot water
1/2 (20-ounce) package light fudge brownie mix
1 teaspoon vanilla extract
2 egg whites
3/4 cup skim milk
2 tablespoons Kahlúa
1 teaspoon instant coffee granules
1 teaspoon vanilla extract
1 (4-ounce) package chocolate instant pudding mix
3 cups light whipped topping, thawed
1 tablespoon Kahlúa
1 teaspoon instant coffee granules

Dissolve 2 teaspoons coffee granules in hot water in bowl. Stir in brownie mix, 1 teaspoon vanilla and egg whites; mix well. Spoon into 9-inch pie plate sprayed with nonstick cooking spray. Bake at 325 degrees for 22 minutes. Cool on wire rack.

Combine skim milk, 2 tablespoons Kahlúa, 1 teaspoon coffee granules, 1 teaspoon vanilla and pudding mix in mixer bowl. Beat at medium speed for 1 minute. Fold in 1 1/2 cups whipped topping. Spread evenly over baked layer.

Combine 1 tablespoon Kahlúa and 1 teaspoon coffee granules in bowl, stirring until coffee granules dissolve. Fold in remaining whipped topping. Spread over pie. Garnish with chocolate curls. Serve immediately or store, loosely covered, in refrigerator.

Your may prepare a nonalcoholic version by substituting milk for the Kahlúa in the pudding mixture and warm water for the Kahlúa in the topping.

Julie Hermann, Knoxville, Tennessee

Julie Hermann was named Head Coach of the Lady Vol Volleyball team in 1991. In 1993, she led the Lady Vols to their first NCAA tournament appearance since 1984. Julie was captain of her 1983 AAU National Championship team and was named College Athlete of the Year.

FRENCH SILK PIE

Serves 12

> 1/2 cup butter
> 3/4 cup sugar
> 2 (1-ounce) squares unsweetened chocolate, melted
> 1 teaspoon vanilla extract
> 2 eggs, at room temperature
> 2 baked (8-inch) pie shells, cooled

Cream butter and sugar in mixer bowl until light and fluffy. Add melted chocolate and vanilla; mix well. Add eggs 1 at a time, beating for 5 minutes after each addition.

Spoon into pie shells. Chill until set. Garnish with whipped cream and grated chocolate.

Ann Sherbakoff, Knoxville, Tennessee

HERSHEY PIE

Serves 6

> 1 (8-ounce) Hershey's chocolate candy bar, melted
> 8 ounces whipped topping
> 1 graham cracker pie shell

Blend chocolate and whipped topping in bowl. Spoon into pie shell. Freeze, covered, until firm.

Dorothy Barkley Bryson, Knoxville, Tennessee

This pie was served to the Sherbakoffs in 1960 by Mrs. J.J. Walker. At the time her husband, known as "J.J.", was the treasurer of the university. "We think of their years of contribution to the University each time we serve it. It is now one of our 'standards'."

FUDGE PIE

Serves 6

> **2 eggs, beaten**
> **1/2 cup melted butter**
> **1 teaspoon vanilla extract**
> **1/4 cup flour**
> **1 cup sugar**
> **1/4 cup baking cocoa**
> **1 unbaked (9-inch) pie shell**

Combine eggs and butter in bowl; mix well. Stir in vanilla. Add mixture of flour, sugar and baking cocoa; mix well. Spoon into pie shell.

Bake at 325 degrees for 25 minutes or until set.

Greg McMichael

Greg McMichael pitched for the Volunteer baseball team from 1986 to 1988. He was a seventh-round choice by the Cleveland Indians and was signed as a free-agent by the Braves in 1991. He rose to prominence with a stellar 1993 season in which he had 19 saves, the most by a National League rookie since 1986. He was the Tennessee Sports Hall of Fame's 1994 Professional Athlete of the Year.

CHOCOLATE CHIP PIES

Serves 12

> **1 cup chopped pecans**
> **1 cup chocolate chips**
> **2 unbaked (9-inch) pie shells**
> **1/2 cup butter or margarine, softened**
> **4 eggs, beaten**
> **1 cup sugar**
> **1 cup corn syrup**

Sprinkle pecans and chocolate chips evenly over bottoms of pie shells. Combine butter, eggs, sugar and corn syrup in bowl; mix well. Spoon into prepared pie shells.

Bake at 300 degrees for 40 to 45 minutes or until set.

■ This is a favorite dessert of Doug Dickey, the Athletic Director at the University of Tennessee.

Mrs. John Guthrie, Knoxville, Tennessee

PEANUT BUTTER PAN PIE

Serves 24

1/4 cup margarine, softened
1 2/3 cups chocolate wafer crumbs
1 cup chunky peanut butter
8 ounces cream cheese, softened
1 cup milk
2 cups confectioners' sugar
16 ounces whipped topping
2 egg whites
1/2 cup sugar
2 tablespoons baking cocoa
6 tablespoons butter
2/3 cup semisweet chocolate chips

Mix margarine and wafer crumbs in bowl. Press evenly over bottom of 9x13-inch baking pan or two 8x8-inch baking pans.

Cream peanut butter and cream cheese in mixer bowl until light and fluffy. Add milk and confectioners' sugar; mix well. Fold in whipped topping. Spread in prepared pan.

Combine egg whites, sugar and cocoa in double boiler. Cook over hot water until smooth, beating constantly. Add the butter 1 tablespoon at a time, beating constantly until blended. Stir in the chocolate chips. Drizzle over prepared layers.

You may substitute crumbled chocolate sandwich cookies for the first layer.

Mary Jo Baldwin Dougherty, Camden, Tennessee

STRAWBERRY PIES

Serves 12

8 ounces cream cheese, softened
2 baked (9-inch) pie shells
2 quarts fresh strawberries
2 cups sugar
6 tablespoons cornstarch
2 tablespoons lemon juice
Several drops of red food coloring
8 ounces whipped topping

Spread cream cheese evenly over bottoms of pie shells. Arrange 2 cups of the strawberries in each pie shell.

Reserve several strawberries for garnish. Mash remaining strawberries in saucepan. Stir in sugar, cornstarch, lemon juice and food coloring.

Cook for 6 minutes or until thickened, stirring constantly. Let stand until cool. Pour over strawberries; spread with whipped topping. Top with reserved strawberries. Chill until serving time.

Pam Wallace, Jackson, Tennessee

Pam's son, Randy Wallace, graduated from The University of Tennessee at Knoxville. "He was not the football quarterback of the same name but enjoyed the fame. Many times, when he is introduced, people comment about what a great quarterback he was! Sometimes we don't correct them!"

PERSIMMON CUSTARD PIE

Serves 6

- 1/2 cup flour
- 2 cups sugar
- 1/2 teaspoon salt
- 1 1/2 teaspoons allspice
- 1/2 teaspoon baking soda
- 2 cups persimmon pulp
- 2 eggs, beaten
- 1 cup milk
- 1/2 cup melted butter
- 2 teaspoons vanilla extract
- 1 unbaked (9-inch) pie shell

Combine the flour, sugar, salt, allspice and baking soda in a bowl; mix well. Stir in persimmon pulp, eggs, milk, butter and vanilla. Spoon into pie shell.

Bake at 300 degrees for 1 hour and 10 minutes.

Jimmy Hahn, Charlottesville, Virginia

Jimmy Hahn is a retired U.S. Army Lieutenant Colonel, and is in real estate and development in Charlottesville, Virginia. He loves this "delicious caramel-tasting pie which was a favorite of mine as a boy during the 1940's when visiting my grandmother, Liz Hahn, on her farm in Cabarras County, North Carolina. I still have memories of listening to the Tennessee Volunteers on January 1, 1945, in the Rose Bowl from a radio in my grandmother's kitchen."

SMOKEY'S GRILL

Through the years, there have been many "Smokey" mascots, all of whom have done the university proud. One, Michael Kennedy, was a mascot for both the Lady Vols and the men's games. The following story is about him.

Smokey the Mascot had a dog-gone rough time getting to the Lady Vols game at the SEC Tournament in Albany, Georgia. It started when Michael Kennedy, the guy in the Smokey costume, missed the bus because the power in University Towers went off and his clock failed to wake him. He already had a flat tire, no money and a missing wallet. He wrote a hot check at a Cumberland Avenue gas station to repair the tire and fill the gas tank and set out very late. He came dangerously close to running out of gas in Atlanta but struck a deal with a hitchhiker to buy gas for a ride.

He arrived at the arena late in the second half just as the Lady Vols were beginning to whittle down a 10-point deficit against the opponents. The fans went crazy when he arrived and graciously gave Smokey his share of the credit for the ultimate win. Michael was then faced with the problems of getting home with no money and facing a summons from Pat Summitt, who was pointing that "infamous Pat finger" at him. Summitt, however, not only thanked Smokey for his support, but took up a collection for the hound dog to get home. As Michael says, "The Lady Vols are so much fun to be with. The Lady Vols are like a big family."

Michael graduated with a degree in Child and Family Studies from the College of Human Ecology in 1994. He has now fulfilled his dream of turning pro and is the Forty Niners' mascot in San Francisco. After appearing at the 1995 Super Bowl, Michael wrote, "I haven't had to get off the playground yet!"

PUNCH DOWN THE COMMODORES HATCH

Serves 20

    3 family-size tea bags
    2 cups boiling water
    1/2 cup sugar
    1 cup boiling water
    1 (6-ounce) can frozen orange juice concentrate
    1 (6-ounce) can frozen pineapple juice concentrate
    1 (6-ounce) can frozen lemonade concentrate
    1 (6-ounce) can frozen limeade concentrate

Steep tea bags in 2 cups boiling water for 15 minutes; remove tea bags. Dissolve sugar in 1 cup boiling water. Combine tea, sugar mixture and juice concentrates in 1-gallon container. Add enough water to fill container; mix well. Serve over ice.

John Van Mol, Nashville, Tennessee

Michael says that, "Through all my five years of doing Smokey/Smokette and being a poverty-stricken student, I ate a lot, a lot, a lot of pasta, ramen noodles and rice! On game days, I'd rise about 6:00 A.M. and eat my macaroni for the day. Then I'd go down to the stadium to watch Dr. Julian lead the band through practice. I MISS YOU GUYS!"

SMOKEY'S PRE-GAME PASTA

Serves 8

    1 (16-ounce) package elbow macaroni, cooked,
        drained
    1/4 cup finely chopped onion
    1/4 cup chopped pimento
    1 pound Cheddar cheese, shredded
    1 cup mayonnaise
    1 (4-ounce) can chopped mushrooms
    1 (10-ounce) can cream of mushroom soup

Combine macaroni, onion, pimento, cheese, mayonnaise, mushrooms and soup in bowl; mix well. Spoon into buttered baking dish.

Bake at 300 degrees for 25 to 30 minutes or until bubbly and heated through. Serve hot.

Michael Kennedy, San Francisco, California

251

RAZORBACK BARBECUE

Serves 12

 **2 (6-pound) bone-in pork shoulder picnic roasts, skin
  removed**
 12 cloves of garlic
 1 cup white vinegar
 2 cups white wine
 1 teaspoon coarse salt
 3¹/₂ cups white wine or vinegar
 1 tablespoon cayenne pepper
 1 tablespoon each honey and molasses
 2 teaspoons dry mustard
 ¹/₂ teaspoon black pepper
 ³/₄ cup prepared barbecue sauce
 Coarse salt and freshly ground black pepper to taste

Place roasts, garlic, vinegar and 2 cups wine in very deep nonreactive stockpot. Add water to cover by 2 inches. Bring to a boil over high heat, skimming occasionally; reduce heat to medium-low. Simmer, partially covered, for 2¹/₂ hours, adding boiling water as necessary to keep meat covered.

Remove roasts to lightly oiled rack set in large roasting pan or place in smoker with mesquite and hickory chips; reserve garlic and ¹/₂ cup cooking liquid.

Mash garlic to a paste with 1 teaspoon coarse salt in bowl. Add 3¹/₂ cups wine, ¹/₄ cup reserved pork cooking liquid, cayenne pepper, honey, molasses, dry mustard and ¹/₂ teaspoon black pepper; mix well. Reserve 1¹/₂ cups sauce for *Mixing Sauce*. Use remaining sauce as *Mopping Sauce* to baste roasts as they cook.

Roast pork at 300 degrees for 2 hours or until meat separates from bone, basting with *Mopping Sauce*. Place roasts on large chopping board. Cover to keep warm and moist.

Discard any fat from roasting pan. Place pan over low heat. Add ¹/₂ cup reserved sauce, stirring to deglaze. Pour into

(continued)

Mopping Sauce. Add remaining 1/4 cup pork cooking liquid. Stir in barbecue sauce. Season with coarse salt to taste. This is the *Mixing Sauce*, a potent potion that will mellow considerably as the barbecue "ripens."

Discard bones and fat from roasts. Tear pork into shreds. Chop finely. Place in large bowl. Stir in half the *Mixing Sauce*. Add remaining *Mixing Sauce* gradually. Cool to room temperature. Chill, tightly covered, for 12 hours or up to 2 days to allow flavor to develop. Let barbecue return to room temperature.

Bake at 300 degrees until heated through. Season with coarse salt and black pepper. Serve with hot pepper sauce and additional barbecue sauce.

Susannah Iacovino, Knoxville, Tennessee

GRILLED PORKER

Serves 6

Meat tenderizer to taste
1 (3-pound) pork tenderloin
1/3 cup red wine vinegar
1/4 cup catsup
1 tablespoon minced garlic or garlic salt
1/4 cup soy sauce
1 tablespoon Worcestershire sauce
1 teaspoon prepared mustard
1/2 teaspoon black pepper
1 teaspoon MSG
1 envelope Italian salad dressing mix, prepared
1/4 cup Italian salad dressing

Sprinkle tenderizer over tenderloin. Combine vinegar, catsup, garlic, soy sauce, Worcestershire sauce, prepared mustard, pepper, MSG and salad dressing in shallow dish; mix well. Add tenderloin. Marinate in refrigerator for 6 to 8 hours.

Place on middle rack of grill over low heat. Grill for 30 minutes, turning every 5 minutes.

Holly Warlick, Knoxville, Tennessee

Holly Warlick is the first UT woman athlete to have her jersey retired and is now a member of the Lady Vol basketball coaching staff. She was a member of the 1980 U.S. Olympic team.

BARBECUED BULLDOGS

Serves 12

> 2 tablespoons vinegar
> 1 1/2 cups tomato juice
> 2 tablespoons brown sugar
> 2 tablespoons prepared mustard
> 1 teaspoon garlic powder
> 1 1/2 cups barbecue sauce
> 1/4 teaspoon salt
> 1 small onion, chopped
> 1/4 cup catsup
> 1 tablespoon Worcestershire sauce
> 8 wieners, cut into 1-inch lengths

Combine vinegar, tomato juice, brown sugar, mustard, garlic powder, barbecue sauce, salt, onion, catsup and Worcestershire sauce in 1-quart saucepan. Cook over medium heat for 20 minutes. Add wieners. Cook until heated through.

This sauce is better if prepared a day ahead.

Nancy S. Starnes, Knoxville, Tennessee

Nancy's best UT memory is of the Lady Vols' 1991 Final Four in New Orleans. "We defeated Virginia in the last few seconds of the game. Pat got Tyler, walked over, and held him up to all the fans hanging in the rafters. There was not a dry eye in that section!"

SMOKED WILDCAT RIBS

Serves 8

> 6 to 8 pounds fresh wildcat or pork ribs
> Crushed red pepper to taste
> 6 (12-ounce) cans inexpensive beer or nonalcoholic beer
> 4 ounces good Scotch whiskey

Rub ribs with red pepper and place in large container with lid. Add beer and whiskey. Marinate, covered, in refrigerator for 8 hours or longer.

Pour marinade into porcelain pan of smoker. Add ribs to smoker. Smoke for 4 hours or until tender, using about 10 pounds of charcoal and adding wood chips occasionally.

Jim McKinney, Knoxville, Tennessee

GRILLED SPICED GAMECOCKS

Serves 5

5 (1- to 1½-pound) Cornish game hens
2 tablespoons paprika
2 tablespoons chili powder
4 teaspoons garlic powder
2 teaspoons onion powder
1 teaspoon celery salt
½ teaspoon salt
½ teaspoon dry mustard
½ teaspoon ground red pepper
⅓ cup vegetable oil

Cut hens into halves lengthwise, cutting through breast bone. Rinse hens; pat dry.

Combine paprika, chili powder, garlic powder, onion powder, celery salt, salt, dry mustard and red pepper in bowl; mix well. Stir in oil. Brush onto hens. Place hens in 2 shallow roasting pans.

Roast, covered, at 375 degrees for 30 minutes. Roast, uncovered, for 45 to 55 minutes longer or until cooked through.

You may grill the hens over medium coals for 30 to 40 minutes or until tender, turning after 20 minutes.

Kathi Wilder, Ripley, Tennessee

Kathi's memories include a wonderful lady named Wymer Carr, the cook at the Phi Gamma Delta fraternity house some years ago. She was much more than a cook to all the brothers and little sisters; she was everyone's mother away from home. "She loved all of us and we loved her. I can still smell her fried chicken—the best anywhere. I know her secret recipe of frying chicken and I am getting better. Bob, Rob and Ben are forever grateful to Wymer!"

JAMAICA JERK WAR EAGLES

Serves 4

1 tablespoon allspice
1 tablespoon thyme
1 1/2 teaspoons cayenne pepper
1 1/2 teaspoons black pepper
1 1/2 teaspoons sage
3/4 teaspoon nutmeg
3/4 teaspoon cinnamon
2 tablespoons salt
2 tablespoons garlic powder
1 tablespoon sugar
1/4 cup olive oil
1/4 cup soy sauce
3/4 cup white vinegar
1/2 cup orange juice
1/4 cup lime juice
1 Scotch bonnet pepper, seeded
1 white onion, finely chopped
3 green onions, finely chopped
4 large chicken breasts

Combine allspice, thyme, cayenne pepper, black pepper, sage, nutmeg, cinnamon, salt, garlic powder and sugar in bowl; mix well. Add olive oil, soy sauce, vinegar, orange juice and lime juice gradually, blending well with wire whisk. Stir in Scotch bonnet pepper, white onion and green onions.

Rinse chicken and pat dry. Add to marinade. Marinate in refrigerator for 1 hour or longer; drain, reserving marinade.

Grill chicken for 6 to 8 minutes on each side, basting with reserved marinade. Heat leftover marinade to serve with chicken.

Chicken may be shredded like barbecue after grilling.

Jim and Glenda Bobo, Knoxville, Tennessee

CUT-THE-GATORS-DOWN-TO-SHRIMP KABOBS

Serves 8

4 oranges
1 pound bacon
2 (8-ounce) cans sliced pineapple
1 pound shrimp, peeled, deveined
2 green bell peppers, coarsely chopped
2 large sweet onions, coarsely chopped
1 (8-ounce) bottle honey-flavored barbecue sauce

Cut unpeeled oranges into halves; cut halves into quarters. Cut bacon slices into halves. Cut pineapple slices into thirds.

Wrap 1 piece of bacon around 1 shrimp and 1 piece of pineapple; repeat with remaining bacon, shrimp and pineapple. Thread peppers, onions, shrimp/pineapple, orange, shrimp/pineapple, onions and peppers in order listed onto skewers. Brush with barbecue sauce. Grill for 10 to 15 minutes or until cooked through.

Phil Kelley, Arden, North Carolina

According to Phil, "Shrimp Kabobs are great to have before the Florida game, when the real Big Orange will make little shrimp of the Gators! Leftovers are good the next day while watching the playback on the coach's show."

SMOKEY'S REBEL-LIOUS CORN BREAD

Serves 8

1 pound ground beef
1/4 cup vegetable oil
1 recipe thin corn bread batter
1 large onion, chopped
1 (16-ounce) can creamed corn
8 slices Velveeta Mexican hot cheese

Brown ground beef in skillet, stirring until crumbly; drain. Heat oil in 9x13-inch baking pan. Stir into corn bread batter.

Layer half the batter, ground beef, onion, corn, cheese and remaining batter in pan. Bake at 400 degrees for 1 hour.

Paul A. Hopkins, Lewisburg, Tennessee

257

HOLD THAT TIGER BARBECUE SAUCE

Serves 6

    1 onion, finely chopped
    1 clove of garlic, minced
    2 tablespoons butter
    1/4 cup packed brown sugar
    3/4 teaspoon cayenne pepper
    1/2 teaspoon dry mustard
    1 teaspoon salt
    1/2 cup chopped celery or 1/2 tablespoon celery salt
    1 tablespoon each prepared horseradish and vinegar
    1/4 cup each lemon juice and Worcestershire sauce
    1 cup catsup
    1 cup water
    Tabasco sauce and red pepper flakes to taste

Sauté onion and garlic in butter in skillet until lightly browned. Add brown sugar, cayenne pepper, dry mustard, salt and celery; mix well. Stir in horseradish, vinegar, lemon juice, Worcestershire sauce, catsup and water.

Simmer for 15 minutes. Adjust "hot" to taste, using Tabasco sauce and red pepper flakes.

Dottie McKinney, Knoxville, Tennessee

UT

Dolores Bettis tells us that Marvin and Nina Everett were part of the "Vol Navy". Years ago, when they lived next to Dr. Joe Bealls, they decided to take their four children to the UT football game by boat rather than by car.

ALABAMA ELEPHANT STEW

Serves 2000

Cut 1 medium elephant into bite-sized pieces. Combine with brown gravy in very large pot. Add vegetables, salt and pepper. Cook over kerosene fire at 450 degrees for several weeks. If you have more guests than expected, add two rabbits, but do this only if needed, since most people do not like hare in their stew.

■ If the elephant is from Alabama, remove the red sweater first and throw it in the fire immediately.

Dolores H. Bettis, Jefferson City, Tennessee
Sherry King Boatright, Kingsport, Tennessee

UT

THE ORANGE PEEL

It's football time in Tennessee, which explains why one young woman has her face painted with an orange on one side and the letters "UT" on the other. As she bounces along the streets of Knoxville, shouts of "Vols! Vols!" fall around her like thunder from the sky.

Why do we come? Why schedule our lives around ten fleeting weeks beginning around Labor Day and ending in early December, or later, if there's a bowl game?

We come because in a time of bewildering change, this is the place where the band still strolls onto the football field trilling Pee Wee King's "Tennessee Waltz" in march time as a blue-tick coon hound and a guy in a Davy Crockett get-up pace the sidelines. We come because it's the only place where everyone can wear the colors of pumpkin and marshmallow and feel fashionable, where even orange boots are okay. We come because, of all the schools that adore the color orange, this is the one whose alumni threw a Bicentennial Ball where "Orange Tie" was required. Most of all, we come because this football ritual is part of something we don't want to lose, no matter how long ago we took off cap and gown and left Knoxville for cities all over the map.

Excerpted from an article by Texas writer Michelle Medley in American Way Magazine.

These recipes have been carefully edited in a style that allows approximate nutritional values to be computed. Persons with dietary or health problems or whose diets require close monitoring should not rely solely on the nutritional information provided; they should consult their physicians or a registered dietitian for specific information.

Nutritional information for these recipes is computed from information derived from many sources, including materials supplied by the United States Department of Agriculture, computer databanks, and journals in which the information is assumed to be in the public domain. Because of new products and changes in familiar products, as well as the trend to supply more information on packages, we strongly urge you to read package labels.

Abbreviations for Nutritional Profiles

Cal — Calories	Fiber — Dietary Fiber	Sod — Sodium
Prot — Protein	T Fat — Total Fat	g — Grams
Carbo — Carbohydrates	Chol — Cholesterol	mg — Milligrams

Measurements and Guidelines for Nutritional Profiles

1. **Measurements**—All volume measurements are level.

2. All **eggs** are large.

3. **Optional Ingredients** are not included in the profile. Ingredients without measurements that are listed in the nature of "serve withs" or garnishes, i.e. corn chips with dips or parsley sprigs, are not included in the profile.

4. **To Taste**—Salt and other seasonings or ingredients to taste have not been included in the nutritional profile.

5. **Alternative Ingredients**—If a choice of ingredients has been given, the profile reflects the first option.

6. **Variable Amounts**—If a choice of amounts or variable amounts have been given, i.e. 3 to 4 cups flour, the profile reflects the greater amount.

7. **Flour**—Unless otherwise specified, all flour is unsifted all-purpose flour.

8. **Marinades**—The profile has been based on the entire amount of marinade since it is impossible to determine the amount absorbed by the food during marinating or cooking.

9. **Dairy Products**—The percentage of fat in commercial products may vary across the country to suit regional tastes and state laws. In this book, unless otherwise specified, the following guidelines were used for analysis:

Product	Butterfat Content
whole milk	3.5%
low-fat milk	1.0%
whipping cream	37.6%
half-and-half	11.7%
cottage cheese, cream-style	4.2%
cottage cheese, dry curd	<1.0%
yogurt	3.5%

   The profile for cheeses is not based on low-fat or low-sodium versions currently available. If these versions are used, make the proper adjustments in the profile by using the label information. Yogurt is plain, produced from whole milk. See carton for additional information.

10. **Fats**—Oils and shortening used in recipes and profiles are vegetable oils and hydrogenated vegetable shortening made from vegetable oils. Butter and margarine are regular, not whipped or pre-softened products.
    Whenever large amounts of shortening or oil are used for frying, the profile does not include the shortening or oil since it is impossible to determine the amount that would be absorbed by the food.

11. **Prepared Foods**—Foods such as canned soups are generic averages rather than brand-specific or dietetic versions now entering the marketplace. Such ingredients as breads and pie crusts are generic averages. When using special diet or especially rich versions, be sure to recognize that the nutritional profile information supplied must be altered.

Page #	Recipe Title (Approx Per Serving)	Cal	Prot (g)	Carbo (g)	T Fat (g)	% Cal From Fat	Chol (mg)	Fiber (g)	Sod (mg)
11	Bacon Wraps	82	2	4	6	69	9	<1	187
11	Sausage Muffins	252	10	15	17	60	28	1	745
12	Mushroom Turnovers	82	1	5	6	69	22	<1	124
13	Strawberries with Spices	96	<1	17	<1	2	0	1	3
13	Tennessee Caviar	70	2	8	4	46	0	3	396
14	Pineapple Cheese Ball	210	4	6	20	83	42	1	437
14	Crab Canapés	59	2	4	4	60	9	<1	137
15	Orange Fluff	140	3	28	3	15	8	2	33
15	Spinach Dip	226	4	17	17	64	18	1	1532
16	Elegant Salad	165	7	5	13	70	10	1	437
16	Spiced Peach Salad	243	2	37	11	39	10	1	99
17	Eggs and Chipped Beef	342	20	12	24	63	334	1	1056
18	Upside-Down Ham Casserole	249	8	35	8	30	16	1	530
19	Egg and Ham Casserole	251	17	7	17	61	241	<1	957
20	Tennessee Spring Brunch Casserole	326	21	25	15	39	198	3	841
21	Sausage and Cheese Casserole	248	11	21	16	52	48	1	907
21	Sausage and Egg Brunch	375	20	11	27	66	229	<1	974
22	Vol Guest Breakfast	221	13	7	15	63	164	<1	663
22	Vol's Real-Man Quiche	440	16	14	36	73	187	1	591
23	Souper Easy Quiche	290	13	16	20	61	133	1	575
23	Artichoke and Chicken Casserole	498	27	14	38	67	90	1	1447
24	Chicken and Crab Meat Casserole	316	25	8	19	53	181	1	656
25	Crab Meat Breakfast Casserole	325	24	11	20	56	230	<1	650
25	Seafood Casserole	289	9	9	25	76	71	1	409
26	Saturday Morning High-Test Scrambled Eggs	312	16	13	22	63	335	3	302
27	Garlic Grits	338	8	22	25	66	106	2	800
28	Hominy Casserole	346	7	42	17	44	13	3	1335
29	Pineapple Casserole	335	7	43	16	42	20	1	275
29	Buttermilk Biscuits	162	3	18	9	50	1	1	133
30	Koffee Kuchen	339	5	48	15	39	84	1	208
31	Sour Cream and Cinnamon Coffee Cake	273	3	32	15	50	64	1	190
32	Apple Pecan Bread	285	4	41	12	38	21	2	254
33	Banana Nut Loaf	327	4	44	16	42	42	1	309
33	Butter Brickle Bread	163	2	20	8	46	36	<1	179
34	Zucchini Bread	269	4	37	12	40	32	1	208
35	Date Nut Muffins	131	3	22	4	27	18	3	95
36	Orange-Pecan Waffles	925	11	97	58	55	169	3	991
37	Corn Bread Waffles	218	5	18	14	57	28	1	367

Page #	Recipe Title (Approx Per Serving)	Cal	Prot (g)	Carbo (g)	T Fat (g)	% Cal From Fat	Chol (mg)	Fiber (g)	Sod (mg)
37	Parmesan Cheese Rolls	145	4	15	8	48	14	1	278
38	Homemade Cinnamon Rolls	199	3	33	6	26	19	1	158
39	Orange Dessert Loaf	317	4	42	15	42	68	<1	284
40	Big Orange Date Cake	506	5	84	18	32	34	3	256
41	Japanese Fruit Pie	294	3	37	17	49	76	2	106
41	Lemon Chess Pie	350	4	50	16	39	96	<1	240
42	Tennessee Treats	290	5	60	4	13	35	2	154
45	Cheese Crispies	164	4	11	12	64	12	<1	283
45	Cheese Wafers	39	1	2	3	73	7	<1	47
46	Party Mix	67	2	5	5	61	4	1	50
46	Tailgate Deviled Eggs	73	3	1	6	78	109	<1	117
47	Zucchini Appetizers	141	4	7	11	68	59	1	248
47	Tailgate Wings	142	10	6	9	55	29	<1	263
48	Miniature Chicken Puffs	223	9	13	15	61	96	<1	420
49	Mongolian Meat Sticks[1]	142	12	5	8	51	28	<1	321
50	Curried Ham Spread	78	6	2	5	61	22	<1	344
50	Pineapple-Pecan Cheese Ball	83	1	2	8	83	17	<1	124
51	Chile Cheese Log	107	4	1	10	80	31	<1	189
51	Layered Nacho Dip	163	6	11	11	59	23	3	566
52	Crunchy Cheese Ball	176	9	2	15	77	36	<1	505
52	Chile and Olive Dip	32	<1	3	2	64	0	1	178
53	Stuffed Cheese Bread	258	11	19	16	54	45	1	578
53	Tailgate Food	Nutritional profile for this recipe is not available.							
54	Rocky Top Joy Juice	35	<1	9	<1	1	0	<1	1
54	Hot Cider Punch	69	<1	18	<1	1	0	<1	2
55	Tailgate Tea Punch	373	1	95	<1	<1	0	1	3
55	Cheese Soup	250	9	9	20	72	45	1	428
56	Gumbo	871	51	63	44	46	123	2	2410
58	Eight-Layer "T" Salad	274	12	17	19	60	39	5	614
59	Chicken Salad	478	22	9	40	75	82	1	378
59	Broccoli Delight Salad	268	6	23	19	59	12	3	178
60	Corn Bread Salad	298	9	30	16	48	54	2	858
60	Shoe Peg Salad	166	3	25	7	37	0	3	239
61	Summer Potato Salad	361	3	24	30	72	22	2	612
62	Tatum Rolls	381	16	23	25	59	79	1	588
63	Go Vols Big Wheel Sandwich	436	21	30	25	53	51	<1	1024
63	Pepperoni Rolls	330	16	21	20	55	50	1	749
64	Black Beans and Rice	229	10	25	10	40	4	9	74

Page #	Recipe Title (Approx Per Serving)	Cal	Prot (g)	Carbo (g)	T Fat (g)	% Cal From Fat	Chol (mg)	Fiber (g)	Sod (mg)
65	Baked Beans	225	7	41	5	20	12	7	661
66	Refrigerator Rolls	72	1	10	3	38	8	<1	40
67	Granny Ruby's Sour Cream Pound Cake	404	5	59	17	37	117	1	178
68	Chocolate Cream Cheese Cupcakes	170	2	22	9	45	19	1	110
69	Caramel Candy	180	1	35	5	22	3	0	62
69	Brickle Bars	234	3	30	12	45	25	1	224
70	Moist Brownies	239	2	31	13	47	12	1	141
71	Peanut Butter Brownies	362	6	51	17	40	24	1	318
72	Chess Squares (Ooey-Gooeys)	242	2	36	10	38	37	<1	220
73	Cocoa Chip Cookies	89	1	12	4	43	7	1	24
74	Gingersnaps	76	1	12	3	35	4	<1	72
75	Magic Mocha Drops	127	1	18	6	44	11	<1	111
76	Oatmeal Chocolate Chip Cookies	181	3	25	9	42	14	2	139
79	Baked Mushrooms Stuffed with Crab Imperial	74	3	2	6	74	26	<1	91
80	Stuffed Mushrooms	109	3	2	10	81	23	<1	156
81	Festive Cheese Mold	226	5	11	19	72	25	1	228
81	Shrimp and Cheese Pâté	66	7	4	3	35	34	<1	321
82	Seafood Fiesta Dip	139	5	6	12	73	22	1	268
83	Seafood Soup	227	22	12	9	33	136	3	757
84	Elegant Wild Rice Soup	263	7	21	17	58	15	2	722
85	Skybox Chili	588	45	44	27	40	126	11	1276
86	Fruity Chicken Salad	545	35	41	29	46	101	5	173
86	Nectarine Buffet Salad[1]	211	3	28	12	46	0	5	30
87	Pasta Salad Roma	477	16	33	32	60	38	2	1103
88	Tennessee Tortellini Salad	333	12	31	19	51	36	1	523
88	Zesty Pasta Salad	709	18	55	47	59	53	3	1508
89	Roasted Potato Salad with Green Beans and Red Onion	325	5	43	16	43	0	6	104
90	Bleu Cheese Potato Salad	245	8	24	13	48	82	2	728
91	Half-Time Beef Sandwiches	485	33	45	18	35	89	3	547
91	The Bama Surprise	493	40	13	24	44	112	2	94
92	Hungarian Cabbage Rolls	447	38	21	23	47	183	3	920
93	Lasagna with Four Cheeses	698	42	40	41	53	145	3	1581
94	Chicken Courtney	Nutritional profile for this recipe is not available.							
95	Seafood Delight	506	40	24	29	51	151	5	2253
96	Battered Fried Shrimp[2]	273	31	27	4	13	277	1	555
97	Star-Spangled Baked Shrimp	541	31	16	33	54	260	3	1254
98	Seafood Casserole	385	29	12	25	58	193	1	719
99	Asparagus Casserole	464	11	27	34	66	24	1	957

Page #	Recipe Title (Approx Per Serving)	Cal	Prot (g)	Carbo (g)	T Fat (g)	% Cal From Fat	Chol (mg)	Fiber (g)	Sod (mg)
100	Broccoli-Stuffed Tomatoes	243	11	12	18	65	28	3	336
101	Fresh Mushroom Casserole	535	19	29	39	65	113	2	1070
102	Ratatouille	112	2	12	7	54	0	3	284
103	Rolls for "Ham Biscuits"	89	2	13	3	33	6	<1	33
104	Fresh Apple Cake	517	4	54	33	55	40	2	267
105	Mocha Brownie Torte Cake	362	3	40	23	55	41	1	81
106	Blue Ribbon Carrot Cake	601	6	71	34	50	88	2	395
108	Congo Bars	84	1	12	4	42	9	<1	33
108	Filled Cannoli	295	11	37	12	35	23	2	41
109	Strawberry Delight	279	2	32	17	52	17	1	79
110	Rocky Top Peanut Butter Pie	622	13	78	30	43	127	2	464
113	Big Orange Shrimp Mold	629	55	12	40	58	504	1	1610
114	Big Orange Punch	293	5	70	<1	1	0	<1	194
114	Orange Nectar Punch	72	1	18	<1	2	0	<1	109
115	Big Orange Slushee Punch	113	<1	29	<1	1	0	<1	9
115	Orange Julius	366	4	85	2	5	8	1	33
116	Orange Crush Soda	557	6	88	18	29	73	<1	174
116	Big Orange Apricot Salad	171	2	22	9	46	1	1	58
117	Big Orange Salad	238	2	36	11	41	9	1	141
117	Big Orange Gelatin Salad	182	4	22	9	43	13	<1	107
118	Mandarin Orange Salad	293	5	50	10	29	0	2	245
119	Big Orange Chicken Salad	465	17	14	39	74	55	1	858
119	Orange and White Chicken	327	31	22	13	36	103	1	240
120	Orange Nuggets	306	2	45	15	41	0	4	480
121	Apricot Orange Bread	232	4	42	6	23	24	2	241
122	Orange Blossom Muffins	222	3	32	10	39	20	1	264
123	Orange Yogurt Coffee Cake	366	5	68	9	21	28	2	446
123	Pumpkin Muffins	880	10	106	49	49	106	4	244
124	Pumpkin Bread	197	2	30	8	34	27	1	120
125	Mandarin Orange Dessert	431	6	67	17	34	37	<1	184
125	Orange Sherbet	195	6	40	2	9	9	<1	101
126	Big Orange Cake	480	4	58	27	49	59	1	317
127	Mandarin Orange Cake	418	5	59	19	40	72	1	532
128	Orange Cake	397	4	67	14	30	36	2	196
129	Orange Slice Cake	738	7	117	28	34	61	4	265
130	Tangy Orange Cake	310	4	69	3	9	41	1	266
131	Tennessee Orange Cake	397	4	60	17	37	73	1	430
132	Big Orange Pound Cake	760	10	114	41	48	208	1	382

Page #	Recipe Title (Approx Per Serving)	Cal	Prot (g)	Carbo (g)	T Fat (g)	% Cal From Fat	Chol (mg)	Fiber (g)	Sod (mg)
133	Orange-Glazed Pound Cake	850	9	148	26	27	72	3	138
134	Creamy Orange Pound Cake	464	6	56	24	47	95	1	301
135	Orange Sponge Cake	116	2	25	1	7	35	<1	90
136	Sweet Orange Nuggets	89	1	15	3	27	13	<1	71
137	Orange Wafer Balls	78	1	12	3	36	4	<1	20
138	Big Orange Bars	104	1	16	4	36	11	1	55
139	Big Orange Cookie Bars	307	4	50	10	30	19	1	259
140	Big Orange Amber Cookies	516	7	84	18	30	22	3	115
140	Orange Crinkles	94	1	12	5	45	12	<1	96
141	Orange Slice Coconut Cookies	107	1	19	3	24	9	<1	54
142	Big Orange Chess Pie	487	6	54	28	52	147	1	351
142	Mandarin Orange Pie	590	7	71	33	49	13	2	298
143	Tangy Big Orange Pie	521	7	75	23	39	29	1	317
143	Big Orange Summer Pie	280	3	35	15	47	0	<1	167
144	Orange Surprise Tarts	282	4	32	17	51	67	2	111
147	Cheese Straws	28	1	2	1	47	4	<1	59
147	Un-Offensive Cheese Ball	108	4	2	10	80	31	<1	223
148	Bagelroonies	578	29	43	32	50	74	3	1517
148	Rocky Top Bread[2]	55	1	8	2	29	14	1	129
149	Clarksville Eggnog	612	14	39	21	30	303	0	163
150	Old College Inn Black Bean Gumbo	355	20	51	9	21	22	17	208
151	Beef Burger Soup	288	20	19	15	47	67	4	1457
152	Company Chili	222	20	24	6	24	37	7	1222
152	Hodgepodge	263	19	24	11	35	48	5	853
153	Old South Brunswick Stew	307	44	10	10	30	119	1	281
153	Sherried Beef	330	33	6	17	48	103	<1	958
154	Meat Loaf	276	21	7	18	58	94	1	264
155	Mexican Dinner	291	23	21	14	41	67	4	2040
156	Lasagna	810	61	50	40	45	182	5	1730
157	Spaghetti Meat Sauce	192	11	16	10	45	30	2	866
158	Orange Pork Chops with Rice	291	26	25	9	28	72	1	439
158	Baked Chicken and Tamales	471	33	25	27	52	113	3	1285
159	Spiced Roast Chicken	700	63	30	31	40	229	5	299
160	Chicken Casserole	598	26	40	37	56	70	2	1213
161	Hot Chicken Salad	353	21	14	24	61	164	2	775
162	Maryland Crab Cakes[2]	178	17	5	10	51	117	<1	354
163	Crawfish Casserole	614	26	25	46	67	152	3	2193
163	Lobster Sauce for Pasta	165	14	8	9	48	54	2	741

Page #	Recipe Title (Approx Per Serving)	Cal	Prot (g)	Carbo (g)	T Fat (g)	% Cal From Fat	Chol (mg)	Fiber (g)	Sod (mg)
164	Casserole Saint Jacques	738	47	32	42	52	313	2	1499
165	Fiery Cajun Shrimp	563	27	10	48	74	361	2	1979
165	Penne Julia	988	41	91	49	46	127	3	1620
166	Broccoli and Walnut Primavera	608	14	53	40	57	3	5	566
167	Spinach Maria	319	18	11	24	66	72	2	841
168	Spinach-Stuffed Tomatoes	154	6	11	11	61	25	3	259
169	Grits Fritters[2]	207	6	12	15	63	60	1	477
170	Riz Biscuits	162	3	20	7	42	11	1	96
171	Hearty Cheesy Beef Corn Bread	525	25	39	31	52	144	3	860
172	Corn Light Bread	214	4	44	2	8	3	1	296
172	Daring Dates	Nutritional profile for this recipe is not available.							
173	Dirt Cake	889	11	117	44	44	44	3	1147
173	Earthquake Cake	416	3	58	20	43	31	1	401
174	Hershey Cake	546	4	105	14	23	74	1	326
175	Six-Flavor Pound Cake	291	3	40	13	41	67	<1	165
176	Regas Red Velvet Cake	728	5	88	42	50	173	1	582
177	Snickerdoodles	64	1	9	3	43	6	<1	28
178	Fudge Pies with Chocolate Sauce	370	5	46	20	47	82	1	169
181	Low-Fat Mexican Dip	282	11	56	4	11	4	9	606
181	Mexican Beef Dip	184	12	6	13	64	51	<1	338
182	Broccoli Soup	203	12	14	13	52	79	5	1194
183	Charlie's Diet Chili	272	23	21	11	36	56	7	1623
184	Low-Fat Corn and Potato Chowder	113	3	26	<1	2	0	2	125
185	Fruit Salad	406	2	32	32	69	0	4	805
185	UT Fruit Bowl	143	2	36	1	4	0	3	8
186	Nutty Pineapple Coleslaw	76	4	14	2	18	0	1	59
186	Tomato Aspic	57	6	5	2	27	5	1	301
187	Pasta Salad	255	5	37	10	35	0	2	183
188	Pasta with Black Beans and Artichoke Hearts	266	12	49	3	11	0	7	603
189	Low-Fat Pocket Sandwiches	359	24	20	21	52	59	1	1178
190	Crunchy Chicken Salad	321	15	21	20	56	29	2	340
190	Paprika Chicken	174	26	<1	7	36	72	0	108
191	Big Orange Fish with Shrimp	250	36	11	7	26	182	3	422
192	Whole Wheat Vegetable Lasagna	197	10	16	11	48	20	3	197
193	Vol Veggies	65	3	7	4	48	1	3	37
193	Stuffed Zucchini	29	2	5	1	15	1	2	25
194	Low-Fat Corn Bread	94	3	17	2	19	2	1	296
194	Low-Fat Cake and Fruit	340	7	57	10	26	8	<1	666

Page #	Recipe Title (Approx Per Serving)	Cal	Prot (g)	Carbo (g)	T Fat (g)	% Cal From Fat	Chol (mg)	Fiber (g)	Sod (mg)
195	Chocolate and Amaretto Cheesecake	249	8	31	11	39	35	2	234
196	Fat-Free Brownies	84	2	20	<1	4	0	1	31
196	No-Bake Sweet Bars	297	8	51	12	31	0	8	237
199	Sunday Barbecued Chicken and Vegetable Soup	Nutritional profile for this recipe is not available.							
199	Vegetarian Spaghetti Sauce	138	3	18	8	52	0	5	90
200	Big Orange Scottish Spaghetti Sauce	248	18	24	10	36	42	6	1558
201	Press Box Meat Loaf	317	28	16	17	46	147	1	506
202	Bologna Sandwich Spread	398	13	6	36	81	97	<1	813
202	Spam and Rice	268	10	21	16	54	0	1	748
203	Fried Chicken	Nutritional profile for this recipe is not available.							
204	Grand Lagoon Stuffed Flounder	742	53	51	36	44	276	2	2937
205	Curried Shrimp	389	21	33	18	51	177	1	860
206	Kesling Korn	Nutritional profile for this recipe is not available.							
207	Big Orange Sweet Potatoes	196	3	37	5	22	8	4	159
208	Fiesta Squash Casserole	294	13	24	18	53	36	4	1139
209	Cottage Cheese Croquettes[2]	370	18	41	15	36	83	3	920
210	Autumn Fruit Salsa	54	1	14	<1	6	0	2	2
210	Volunteer Jam	1099	1	284	<1	<1	0	3	276
211	Big Orange Tomato Sauce	Nutritional profile for this recipe is not available.							
212	Chocolate Crinkle Cookies	96	1	15	4	35	17	<1	40
213	'Nilla Orange Balls	106	1	15	5	41	7	<1	62
214	Lemon Meringue Pie	379	4	64	13	30	87	1	175
217	Easy Apple Dumplings	551	4	62	33	53	32	1	571
218	Apple Pudding Soufflé	235	6	32	10	38	104	1	236
219	Banana Pudding	374	6	63	13	29	92	1	185
220	Blueberry Pizza	386	5	56	17	38	38	2	381
221	Lemon Chiffon Cheesecake	354	5	43	18	46	50	1	303
222	Amaretto Cake	486	6	64	23	42	117	1	308
223	Carrot Cakes	436	4	48	26	53	27	2	132
224	Chocolate-Covered Cherry Cake	418	5	64	18	37	47	2	379
224	Triple Chocolate Cake	316	5	44	16	43	7	2	340
225	Smokey's Mississippi Mud Cake	336	3	55	13	33	46	1	290
226	Time-Saver Chocolate Cake	398	4	53	20	45	62	1	238
227	Chocolate Sheet Cake	527	4	73	26	43	29	2	219
228	Chocolate Peppermint Log	274	4	42	12	36	103	1	105
230	Southern White Chocolate Cake	543	4	63	32	51	102	1	341
231	Coconut Cake	641	5	80	35	48	82	3	301
232	Company Coconut Cake	753	7	80	47	55	82	2	459

Page #	Recipe Title (Approx Per Serving)	Cal	Prot (g)	Carbo (g)	T Fat (g)	% Cal From Fat	Chol (mg)	Fiber (g)	Sod (mg)
233	Grand Marnier Cake	379	5	36	24	55	79	1	212
234	Peach Upside-Down Cake	315	3	61	7	21	70	1	202
235	Butterscotch Icebox Cookies	60	1	8	3	44	7	<1	43
236	Tennessee Gourmet Chocolate Chip Cookies	109	2	15	5	42	8	1	92
237	Easy Chocolate Chip Cookies	128	1	18	6	42	12	1	5
237	Fruit Cookies	182	2	22	10	49	21	1	80
238	Quick Peanut Butter Cookies	105	2	18	4	29	0	1	87
238	Easy Peanut Butter Blossom Cookies	94	2	13	4	40	3	<1	76
239	Peanut Butter Temptations	99	2	11	6	51	11	<1	92
240	Amber Pie	537	7	73	25	41	82	1	344
241	Bob's Favorite Apple Pie	607	5	91	26	38	41	4	326
242	Granny's Butterscotch Pie	478	9	61	23	42	169	1	399
243	Mocha Fudge Pie	274	3	50	6	20	1	<1	323
244	French Silk Pie	294	3	27	20	61	56	1	234
244	Hershey Pie	582	5	67	35	52	8	3	350
245	Fudge Pie	475	5	54	28	52	112	2	341
245	Chocolate Chip Pies	526	5	63	31	50	91	2	297
246	Peanut Butter Pan Pie	311	5	29	21	58	23	1	165
247	Strawberry Pies	458	4	63	22	43	21	3	225
248	Persimmon Custard Pie	696	7	106	29	37	118	2	608
251	Punch Down the Commodores Hatch	80	<1	20	<1	1	0	<1	1
251	Smokey's Pre-Game Pasta	681	23	48	45	59	76	2	882
252	Razorback Barbecue	802	91	8	35	40	321	1	598
253	Grilled Porker[1]	498	41	8	33	61	111	<1	2069
254	Barbecued Bulldogs	166	5	10	12	63	19	1	942
254	Smoked Wildcat Ribs[1]	821	51	9	52	58	208	1	173
255	Grilled Spiced Gamecocks	963	94	5	62	58	298	2	1609
256	Jamaica Jerk War Eagles[1]	378	36	21	18	41	90	2	4310
257	Cut-the-Gators-Down-to-Shrimp Kabobs	253	16	27	10	33	94	3	595
257	Smokey's Rebel-lious Corn Bread	403	21	32	22	48	81	2	788
258	Hold that Tiger Barbecue Sauce	129	1	24	4	28	10	1	1004
258	Alabama Elephant Stew	Nutritional profile for this recipe is not available.							

[1]Nutritional profile for this recipe includes the entire amount of marinade.
[2]Nutritional profile for this recipe does not include oil for deep-frying.

Complete the Order Form, include your check, or credit card information and mail to:

**Tennessee Traditions
P.O. Box 15016
Knoxville, Tennessee 37901**

Checks payable to:
University of Tennessee
Phone Orders: 615-974-1270
FAX Orders to: 615-974-3119

Phone orders call Mon-Fri 9 a.m. - 6 p.m.
Saturday 10 a.m. - 4 p.m.

Refunds must be made within 30 days

METHOD OF PAYMENT:
☐ Discover ☐ MasterCard ☐ Visa ☐ Check or Money Order

Card Number   Exp. Date   Signature (required for Credit Card purchases)

To order *A Slice of Orange* Cookbook
PLEASE PRINT

Name_____
Address_____
City_____ State____ Zip _____
Home Phone ___ - ___ - _____ Day Phone ___ - ___ - _____

QTY.	DESCRIPTION	UNIT PRICE	AMOUNT
	"A Slice of Orange" Cookbook	$19.95	
		Postage & Handling	$5.00/book
		TOTAL	

Complete the Order Form, include your check, or credit card information and mail to:

**Tennessee Traditions
P.O. Box 15016
Knoxville, Tennessee 37901**

Checks payable to:
University of Tennessee
Phone Orders: 615-974-1270
FAX Orders to: 615-974-3119

Phone orders call Mon-Fri 9 a.m. - 6 p.m.
Saturday 10 a.m. - 4 p.m.

Refunds must be made within 30 days

METHOD OF PAYMENT:
☐ Discover ☐ MasterCard ☐ Visa ☐ Check or Money Order

Card Number   Exp. Date   Signature (required for Credit Card purchases)

To order *A Slice of Orange* Cookbook
PLEASE PRINT

Name_____
Address_____
City_____ State____ Zip _____
Home Phone ___ - ___ - _____ Day Phone ___ - ___ - _____

QTY.	DESCRIPTION	UNIT PRICE	AMOUNT
	"A Slice of Orange" Cookbook	$19.95	
		Postage & Handling	$5.00/book
		TOTAL	